CONTENTS 05

US Marine Corps/Sgt Sean Potter

US Marine Corps/Cpl Christian Cortez

US Navy/Matthew Lyall

ISBN: 978 1 83632 007 4
Editor: Mark Ayton
Senior editor, specials: Roger Mortimer
Email: roger.mortimer@keypublishing.com
Cover Design: Steve Donovan
Design: SJmagic DESIGN SERVICES, India
Advertising Sales Manager: Sam Clark
Email: sam.clark@keypublishing.com
Tel: 01780 755131
Advertising Production: Becky Antoniades
Email: Rebecca.antoniades@keypublishing.com

SUBSCRIPTION/MAIL ORDER
Key Publishing Ltd, PO Box 300, Stamford, Lincs, PE9 1NA
Tel: 01780 480404
Subscriptions email: subs@keypublishing.com
Mail Order email: orders@keypublishing.com
Website: www.keypublishing.com/shop

PUBLISHING
Group CEO and Publisher: Adrian Cox

Published by
Key Publishing Ltd, PO Box 100, Stamford, Lincs, PE9 1XQ
Tel: 01780 755131
Website: www.keypublishing.com

PRINTING
Precision Colour Printing Ltd, Haldane, Halesfield 1, Telford, Shropshire. TF7 4QQ

DISTRIBUTION
Seymour Distribution Ltd, 2 Poultry Avenue, London, EC1A 9PU
Enquiries Line: 02074 294000.

We are unable to guarantee the bona fides of any of our advertisers. Readers are strongly recommended to take their own precautions before parting with any information or item of value, including, but not limited to money, manuscripts, photographs, or personal information in response to any advertisements within this publication.

© Key Publishing Ltd 2024
All rights reserved. No part of this magazine may be reproduced or transmitted in any form by any means, electronic or mechanical, including photocopying, recording or by any information storage and retrieval system, without prior permission in writing from the copyright owner. Multiple copying of the contents of the magazine without prior written approval is not permitted.

US NAVY AND MARINE CORPS YEARBOOK 2024

US NAVAL AVIATION VISION 2030-2035

POSTURING

Commander, Naval Air Forces based in San Diego, California, continues to accelerate change through the naval aviation fleet in accordance with the latest doctrine. We look at the aspects of that doctrine most relevant to this publication.

ACCORDING TO THE document *Navy Aviation Vision 2030-2035*: "The National Defense Strategy (NDS) identifies a complex global security environment characterized by overt challenges to the current international order and the resurgence of long-term, strategic competition among nations. It calls for a lethal, agile, resilient, and rapidly deployable force designed to compete against, deter, and win victories over all adversaries. Implementing the Chief of Naval Operations' (CNOs') guidance centred on our core principles of sea control and power projection, and the forward-looking Fleet Design concept, the navy conducts distributed maritime operations (DMO), providing the strong maritime component that the NDS requires. Integral to the NDS, naval aviation is focused on updating current capabilities, bringing new and advanced platforms online, and complementing today's warfighting competency with enhanced tactics and procedures for the high-end fight.

"Carrier Strike Groups (CSGs) — centred on large-deck, nuclear-powered aircraft carriers and their embarked Carrier Air Wings (CVWs) — provide fleet commanders with multi-domain military might. CSGs provide unmatched contributions of lethality, battle space awareness, and mobility to any maritime theatre, ensuring the navy's ability to establish and sustain sea control, achieve maritime superiority, and project power at great distances. The navy's expeditionary fixed and rotary wing, manned and unmanned aircraft constitute the most widely distributed aviation platforms in the world, operating in support of CSGs, expeditionary strike groups (ESGs), and surface ships, providing a broad range of enabling missions."

The document reflects the key concepts deemed necessary to meet the Chief of Naval Operations' vision of a navy that "swarms the sea, delivering synchronized lethal and non-lethal efforts from near and far, on every axis and in every domain."

The vision of Commander, Naval Air Forces', the Air Boss, outlines three key elements — "delivering capability and capacity to win in the great power competition (GPC); generating future readiness across the force; and achieving revolutionary training — to form the framework of naval aviation's future."

Strategic Environment

Outlining the strategic environment, the document states: "The character of maritime warfare is changing rapidly and despite efforts over the last few years, China and Russia continue to work to erode the US Navy's warfighting advantages, which put national objectives in jeopardy. Technological advancements increase the potential for adversaries to track, target, and threaten US Navy ships and aircraft."

Anticipated threat capabilities held by America's adversaries will be more complex, more disruptive, and more lethal, such that by the early 2030s, naval aviation can expect to face:

- An increased People's Liberation Army Navy (PLAN) aircraft carrier inventory.
- Improved People's Liberation Army Air Force (PLAAF) capabilities and capacity that includes fighters, bombers, and special mission aircraft.
- Advanced kill chains (the structure of an attack) that extend over great distances.
- Proliferation of complex threat emitters.

Information Warfare Attacks

Outlining the risk of information warfare attacks, the document says: "In an environment of great power competition, left unchecked, symmetric, and asymmetric threats can impose a high cost by exposing American forces to significant risk. This could jeopardize the US Navy's ability to project power and maintain maritime superiority. Anticipating and staying ahead of these advancements by developing and fielding capable and affordable platforms, weapons and sensors on a relevant timeline is at the forefront of naval aviation priorities."

Above: **An EA-18G Growler assigned to Electronic Attack Squadron 138 (VAQ-138) 'Yellowjackets' flies in formation with a KC-135 Stratotanker over the Pacific Ocean while flying in support of Exercise Valiant Shield.** US Air Force/MSgt Nicholas Priest

FOREWORD

AMERICA'S DEPARTMENT OF the Navy comprises two armed services, the US Marine Corps, and the US Navy. Each service has a large aviation element. The Department of Aviation, US Marine Corps, and Naval Air Forces each command large fleets of aircraft, helicopters, tiltrotors, and unmanned air vehicles.

Naval Air Training Command is mid-course to issuing its request for proposals for the Undergraduate Jet Training System programme which is anticipated to replace the current T-45 platform used for intermediate and advanced jet training of navy and marine corps aviators and flight officers. Three teams look to be bidding, Textron Defense partnered with Leonardo of Italy, Lockheed Martin partnered with Korea Aerospace Industries, and Boeing. We have been able to include the latest on the proposals from both Textron Defense and Lockheed Martin.

Textron Defense is also delivering T-54A aircraft to Training Wing 4 (TAW-4) based at NAS Corpus Christi, Texas as the replacement aircraft for the legacy T-44 Pegasus. The programme is dubbed METS for Multi-Engine Training System and includes a selection of training aids and simulators in addition to T-54A aircraft. The latest details are covered inside.

The growing number of Lockheed Martin F-35 Lightning II stealth fighters continues to inject significant capability to the fleet. This edition includes sections about VMFAT-502, the west coast F-35B training squadron based at MCAS Miramar, and VMFA-542, the first east coast fleet squadron based at MCAS Cherry Point.

In the future, the world's first unmanned, carrier-capable tanker, the MQ-25 Stingray, will join the ranks of carrier air wings. We provide an extensive overview of the type including the latest details from the MQ-25 programme.

Marine Expeditionary Units already deploy onboard US Navy amphibious assault ships equipped with complements of F-35B stealth fighters, AH-1Z gunships, and MV-22B tiltrotors which have transformed the collective capability of a MEU.

Working in partnership, Naval Air Systems Command's H-53 Heavy Lift Helicopters Program office, PMA-261, 2nd Marine Aircraft Wing and Marine Heavy Helicopter Squadron 461 (HMH-461) continue to field the brand-new CH-53K King Stallion. We cover this powerful helicopter in detail which is scheduled to embark on the type's first at-sea deployment with a Marine Expeditionary Unit in 2026.

US Navy and Marine Corps Air Power Yearbook 2024 covers the latest types in service with America's sea services.

Mark Ayton, Editor

An F-35B of VMFA-542, a former AV-8B Harrier II unit.
US Marine Corps/ WO Akeel Austin

CONTENTS

US Navy/Mass Communication Specialist Matthew Nass

06 Doctrine
The latest insights to the concepts of operation and doctrines used by the US Marine Corps and US Navy.

10 M-346N
Textron Defense has partnered with Leonardo to offer its M-346 trainer aircraft as a candidate for the US Navy's Undergraduate Jet Training System.

18 TF-50N
We report on Lockheed Martin's partnership with Korea Aerospace Industries to offer the US Navy's Undergraduate Jet Training System programme its T-50 trainer aircraft.

26 T-44 Pegasus
The T-44 Pegasus is the US Navy's only multi-engine advanced pilot training aircraft. Two squadrons fly the T-44 from NAS Corpus Christi in Texas. Its days are now numbered, so we took the opportunity to cover the aircraft before its sundown.

32 T-54A Multi-Engine Trainer
Textron Aviation Defense won a contract to supply US Naval Training Command with King Air 260 aircraft for the Multi-Engine Training System programme.

40 Keeping the Sting Alive
After 26 years in US Navy fleet service, Naval Air Systems Command continues to develop and support the F/A-18 Super Hornet, now operating in Block III configuration.

46 Stingray
Naval Air Systems Command and Boeing's Phantom Works are developing the carrier-based MQ-25 Stingray autonomous aerial refuelling unmanned air vehicle.

64 Fighting Bengals
Marine All Weather Fighter Attack Squadron 224 (VMFA[AW]-224) 'Fighting Bengals' is the final such squadron in the US Marine Corps' tactical air fleet. Based at Marine Corps Air Station Beaufort, South Carolina, the unit remains busy.

72 The Ace of Spades
Marine Attack Squadron 231 (VMA-231) 'Ace of Spades' is the last but one east coast front line AV-8B Harrier squadron in the 2nd Marine Aircraft Wing.

80 AH-1Z and UH-1Y Training
Marine Light Attack Helicopter Training Squadron 303 (HMLAT-303) 'Atlas' is the only H-1 training squadron in the US Marine Corps. Its home station is Marine Corps Air Station Camp Pendleton, California.

90 Marine Corps Heavy Lift
Mark Ayton spoke with NAVAIR's H-53 programme manager, US Marine Corps Colonel Kate Fleeger about the CH-53K King Stallion.

96 F-35B Pilot Training
Marine Fighter Attack Training Squadron 502 (VMFAT-502) is the US Marine Corps' west coast F-35B fleet replacement squadron. Mark Ayton spoke with the squadron's executive officer about its operations.

106 Fifth-Generation Tigers
Marine Fighter Attack Squadron 542 (VMFA-542) 'Tigers' is the first east coast front line F-35B squadron to stand-up in the 2nd Marine Aircraft Wing.

US NAVY AND MARINE CORPS YEARBOOK 2024

US NAVAL AVIATION VISION 2030-2035

Carrier Air Wing (CVW)

The US Navy's nine CVWs are the primary fighting element of a CSG. Current CVWs will each transition to an Air Wing of the Future (AWoF) by the assignment of Block III F/A-18 Super Hornets, F-35C Lightning IIs, E-2D Advanced Hawkeye aircraft, and MQ-25 Stingrays. According to the document: "The AWoF is designed to be increasingly lethal, survivable, networked, sustainable, and unmanned with autonomous capabilities. Integrated passive and active sensors will provide battlespace awareness for the CSG and fleet commander. An AWoF will be designed to deliver precision effects on many types of targets using next generation aircraft with greater range and speed. Low-observable aircraft, advanced tactical data links, passive targeting, long-range collaborative weapons, increased sensor detection range and identification, high-power, full-spectrum airborne electronic attack, and beyond line-of-sight (BLOS) communications will form the building blocks of future naval integrated strike force. Updated passive detection systems, directed energy weapons for offensive and defensive measures, non-kinetic techniques to influence adversary decision-making, and hypersonic weapons capability to decrease time to kill will be designed to further ratchet up CVW capability.

"Through 2025, the backbone of the CVW will be the Block III F/A-18 Super Hornet featuring reduced signature, infrared search and track (IRST), and increased computing power. The F-35C will serve as a force multiplier for the CSG with the capability to gain critical intelligence and share that information throughout the CSG. Once the Block 4 standard is fully fielded, the F-35C will be able to employ the AGM-154C-1 Joint Standoff Weapon, the AGM-88E Advanced Anti-Radiation Guided Missile Extended Range, and the GBU-53 Small Diameter Bomb II. By using the F-35C's stealth and passive detection capabilities to shape the overall air picture, the survivability and lethality of Block III Super Hornets should be increased.

"The F/A-XX is the strike fighter component within the US Navy's nascent Next Generation Air Dominance

Future Technologies

The use of the latest and nascent technologies is common, not least with the US sea services. Explaining some significant examples, the document says: "Given the rapidly advancing threat, naval aviation must invest in and pursue advanced technologies and concepts of operation to succeed at the operational level of war.

"Naval aviation's advanced technologies include manned-unmanned teaming or MUM-T which reduces risk to manned aircraft assigned to the CVW, while simultaneously increasing capability, capacity, and survivability. Unmanned air systems (UAS) such as the MQ-25 Stingray which will undertake diverse roles with the distributed surface fleet to conduct missions such as aerial refuelling, communications relay, logistics, airborne electronic attack, strike, and intelligence, surveillance, reconnaissance, and targeting. As a tanker with a secondary ISR role, the MQ-25 is designed to increase the reach and lethality of the CVW.

"The MQ-4C Triton UAS is designed to deliver persistent maritime ISR&T using human-machine and autonomous teaming. Propulsion solutions such as variable cycle engines could provide increased speed, range, and endurance while simultaneously providing power and cooling to advanced mission systems. Long-range, high-capacity, and hypersonic weapons will not only extend the air-to-air and surface-to-air reach, but also defeat both manoeuvring air targets and surface-to-air defences. Such capabilities will be achieved using hypersonic weapons, and/or other disruptive technologies such as directed energy weapons. The ability to counter adversary cyber effects and enhance cyber capabilities and platforms. The USS Gerald Ford-class aircraft carriers are being designed to support these and other technologies into the future."

Nuclear-Powered Aircraft Carriers (CVN)

The document outlines the capabilities of US Navy aircraft carriers saying: "Large-deck CVNs are deemed to be the most survivable, agile, resilient, and lethal airfields in operation within today's security environment. Their sheer size can support an air wing with enough aircraft to simultaneously conduct long-range power projection, sea control, and surveillance missions in nearly all environmental conditions and sea states. Nuclear-powered propulsion affords increased space onboard for stores, weapons, aviation fuel and survivability features, space that might otherwise be used for fuel in conventionally-powered vessels. America's CVNs can conduct high-speed transits over great distances and then conduct military operations from 70% of the earth's surface and can do so for extended periods."

(NGAD) family of systems (FoS), which is supposed to eventually replace the Super Hornets. It is meant to be all-singing with longer range and higher speed performance, equipped with passive and active sensors and the capability to employ future long-range weapons. Eventually, F/A-XX aircraft will operate with F-35C Lightning IIs.

"CVW electronic attack capability resides in the EA-18G Growler which already provides the full-spectrum of integrated non-kinetic effects for the air wing and the joint expeditionary force. By September 2024, the first EA-18G squadron will deploy with the ALQ-249 Next Generation Jammer-Mid Band (NGJ-MB). The unit is believed to be Electronic Attack Squadron 133 (VAQ-133) 'Wizards'. The CVW's electronic attack capability has increased since the arrival of the F-35C, an aircraft which complements and augments the Growler."

Outlining the significance of the E-2 command and control aircraft, the document says: "The E-2 Hawkeye aircraft remains a critical element of the CVW. Now in its fourth variant, the E-2D Advanced Hawkeye will remain as the quarterback of the fleet and the linchpin for a CSG's self-defence. Equipped with the APY-9 AESA radar, active and passive sensors, and robust networks and communication capacities, the radar can provide real-time actionable data to aircraft and helicopters on a mission, and to commanders to enable power projection, theatre air and missile defence, and anti-ship missile defence in highly contested environments. In over a decade from now, the navy hopes to employ the E-2D to leverage manned and unmanned teaming; next-generation active, multi-spectral and passive sensors; and enhanced combat identification to provide an integrated fires capability across all domains."

Detailing the rotary wing element of a CVW, the document says: "A CVW's helicopter element is provided by MH-60R and MH-60S Sea Hawks which rely upon speedy and accurate data transfer. To futureproof the helicopters for this requirement, the existing Link-16 datalink will be upgraded to, what's called the concurrent multi-net 4, supported by improved mission computers. Additionally, investment in the Minotaur mission system (which incorporates sensors, radar, command, control, communications, computers, cyber, and intelligence, surveillance, and

reconnaissance equipment) will improve the MH-60R's common operating picture, and increase aircrew situational awareness by enabling robust, cross-platform data sharing. The MH-60R will also receive a downlink capability with an integrated broadcast service (IBS) feed via an upgraded receiver. A digital magnetic anomaly detection (DMAD) system is intended to provide a non-acoustic anti-submarine warfare capability."

This publication features extensive coverage of the MQ-25 Stingray which includes mention of its role in paving the way for unmanned air vehicle operations on an aircraft carrier and manned and unmanned teaming (MUM-T) to extend strike range and enhance manoeuvrability. Continued development of MUM-T will enable sensor information sharing across a distributed force, increasing survivability, reducing risk to manned aircraft, and ensuring weapons capacity.

The document also makes mention of a system called Navy Integrated Fire Control (NIFC) which will continue to integrate sensors and weapons in the CVW with naval surface platform sensors and weapons to enable robust extended-range kill chains in all domains.

Flight Training

As naval aviation's aircraft, weapons, and sensors are modernised, training must also modernise to keep pace with the threat environment. Initiatives to ensure high-end training include Chief of Naval Air Training (CNATRA) recapitalisation; a fleet surrogate strategy; and enhanced Air Wing Fallon facilities.

In 2035, naval aviation will be almost complete with the recapitalisation of three training aircraft categories. These are the TH-73A for rotary and tilt-rotor students; the T-54A for multi-engine aircraft training; and the Undergraduate Jet Training System (UJTS) for fast-jet students. This publication features extensive coverage of the T-54A METS programme and two of the three candidate aircraft which are bidding for UJTS.

US NAVAL AVIATION VISION 2030-2035

Above: **An F-35C Lightning II assigned to Strike Fighter Squadron 125 (VFA-125) 'Rough Raiders' taxies on the flight deck of the aircraft carrier USS *Nimitz* (CVN68).** US Navy/Mass Communication Specialist 3rd Class Jared Mancuso

Fleet Surrogates and Adversaries

The navy is evaluating the concept of fleet surrogate aircraft to train fleet aircrew in less demanding mission sets, probably using the same type selected for the UJTS programme.

In addition to reconfigurable large area displays with the ability to simulate various fleet aircraft, LVC (live, virtual, construct) systems will allow the fleet surrogate to emulate radar and IRST systems. However, the largest benefit to be realised from the fleet surrogate is cost savings. Flight time and training could be accomplished at a fraction of the cost of fleet aircraft while simultaneously reducing some of the flight burden on fleet aircraft.

The type of aircraft selected for the UJTS programme could also potentially be used to fulfil some of the adversary requirements of naval aviation. LVC capabilities coupled with podded or integrated emulation systems capable of providing appropriate waveforms will enable these aircraft to replicate fourth and fifth-generation threats. Such aircraft would replace legacy F-5 adversary aircraft.

Air Wing Fallon Training

The Naval Aviation Warfighting Development Center (NAWDC) based at Naval Air Station Fallon, Nevada is the centre of excellence for naval aviation air combat training and tactics development. Its primary mission is integrated training, both live and virtual, of air wings in the final phase of their work-up training. Its focus is on the tactics, techniques, and procedures tailored to fight and win the high-end fight against peer competitors.

The document says: "To properly prepare aircrew for the anticipated threat, NAWDC continually updates the Fallon Range Training Complex (FRTC) threat emulators, Air Wing Fallon (AWF) syllabi, and its training systems and facilities. NAWDC has expanded the eastern and southern airspace in the FRTC and periodically makes altitude reservations between FRTC, the Utah Test and Training Range (UTTR), and the Nevada Test and Training Range (NTTR), while using LVC training to complement the smaller airspace structure.

"NAWDC's integrated training facility (ITF) enables the full scope of AWF integrated training at the security levels required to employ the full capabilities of the CVW and train for the high-end fight. The ITF also integrates with other navy sites through the navy continuous training environment (NCTE) as well as the US Air Force to enable full joint mission rehearsal, integrated strike group air defence training, AWF mission rehearsal, weapons, and tactics instructor support, TTP development, combatant commander (CCDR) mission rehearsal, and unit-level training.

"Weapons and Tactics Instructors (WTI) who have graduated from one of the NAWDC weapons schools — including TOPGUN — the Air Combat Training Continuum (ACTC) provides a cost-effective and standardized training curriculum to ensure fleet aviators develop and demonstrate the tactical proficiency required to support CCDR intent for the full spectrum of operations."

In conclusion, the navy's fleet of aircraft currently being developed and procured for the 2035 timeline is a mix of: complementary fourth and fifth-generation aircraft; the NGAD FoS; manned and unmanned platforms; and netted sensors and weapons. This arsenal of weapon systems is being designed to decisively defeat increasingly advanced near-peer threats. The navy's intention is to integrate sea-based and land-based aircraft — both manned and unmanned — to provide a persistent, agile, tailorable force with the flexibility and responsiveness to provide a stabilising presence, de-escalate regional tensions, or to use force to impose cost on America's adversaries.

UNDERGRADUATE JET TRAINING SYSTEM

M-346N

Textron Defense has formed a partnership with Leonardo to offer its M-346 trainer aircraft as a candidate for the US Navy's Undergraduate Jet Training System.

NAVAL AIR SYSTEMS Command has issued a Request for Information (RFI) for the Undergraduate Jet Training System (UJTS), which is anticipated to replace the current tandem-seat, carrier capable T-45 Goshawk used for intermediate and advanced jet training of US Navy and US Marine Corps aviators and flight officers. The T-45 aircraft is one component of an integrated training system that includes operations and instrument fighter simulators, academics, and a training integration system.

Discussing the applicability of their M-346 jet trainer to UJTS, Tom Webster, vice president of global sales and strategy for Textron Aviation Defense said: "When we learned of the UJTS, we realised that we weren't going to produce a white sheet aeroplane, so we looked for a potential partner, fortuitously we discovered Leonardo. When we studied the M-346 integrated training system we realised the potent match for the navy's nascent UJTS requirements.

"The US Navy needs a fully integrated training system, not just a great aeroplane, but a system that integrates the live virtual constructive piece around that aircraft, so that the Chief of Naval Training [CNATRA] can tailor its training.

"We can put a nugget pilot, freshly graduated from turboprop training on the

UNDERGRADUATE JET TRAINING SYSTEM

T-6B, into the M-346 for their fast jet training such that three months later, they're very comfortable with that piece, and then do information management training, and create a challenging combination of virtual live and constructive entities to an extent that would challenge a pilot with experience of flying fighter aircraft. In other words, the M-346 integrated training system takes a student from their first jet sortie to experience flying that nearly-replicates flying a fifth- or sixth-generation platform, be part of a large force package, and go to a tanker.

"The M-346 system has already been validated by the Italian Air Force at its international flight training school [IFTS] which is graduating pilots that are then assigned to the F-35. The Italian Air Force has accumulated 100,000 hours on the M-346, it's a proven platform. The bespoke integrated training system allows the customer to create the training environment they require.

"The M-346 performance capabilities are a solid match to the RFI, and in many elements beyond the requirements listed in the RFI. Until a Request for Proposal [RFP] is issued by Naval Air Systems Command, we're working off the RFI and conversations with CNATRA representatives."

Key Aspects

Dave Kindley, a former US Navy F/A-18 pilot and a member of the Textron-Leonardo M-346 team explained three key points about the design's applicability to the UJTS: "Everybody we spoke with at last year's Tailhook symposium [the Tailhook Association is an independent, fraternal, nonprofit organisation internationally recognised as the premier supporter of the aircraft carrier and other sea-based aviation] were interested in the fact that the M-346 has two engines, and how that would mitigate single engine-related issues with the T-45, particularly at Naval Air Station Kingsville caused by the bird activity at the base. The M-346 is the only two-engine aircraft currently in the UJTS competition.

"CNATRA is currently under immense pressure to train the required number of pilots and is trying to take on some of the training burden from the F/A-18 and F-35 fleet replacement squadrons, plus the complexity of the curriculums are harder. We're trying to highlight how the M-346 system plugs into the larger pilot training system. The Italian IFTS has reduced the time to train a pilot which has taken cost out of the operational commands. Pilots graduating from the IFTS are trained in aerial refuelling, night-vision goggles, and low-level flying.

"The M-346 Joint User Group meets annually and provides feedback to Leonardo about required changes, everything from procedures on maintenance to software baselines to configuration of the aeroplane, the aircraft has been evolving for ten years in response to customer inputs, and there are more things coming in response to what we believe the UJTS requirements will be."

Below: A computer-generated image of an M-346N trainer in a light grey colour scheme leads a formation of Naval Air Training Command Beechcraft aircraft, left to right, T-44 Pegasus, T-54A METS, M-346N, T-6B Texan and the T-34C Mentor. Textron Aviation Defense

UNDERGRADUATE JET TRAINING SYSTEM

Precision Landing Mode

Naval Air Systems Command has yet to issue an RFP but is reportedly considering an aircraft that does not have to be carrier capable. Explaining this significant change in naval aviator training, Kindley said: "The US Navy uses a system initially called Magic Carpet which is now called Precision Landing Modes or PLM. When a pilot rolls the aircraft wings level behind the ship, you're in a straight line for about 18 seconds, we call that the groove. Before PLM, a typical aviator would make between 200 and 300 corrections, with PLM, proficient aviators are making less than 20 and often less than 10, it has changed the game for getting aboard a ship.

"To train pilots, CNATRA needs the use of aircraft carriers. Aircraft carriers are primarily used to train up an air wing or they are deployed. Training, whilst important, is not a priority and there are a lot of competing priorities. Some classes are held hostage to the schedule of an aircraft carrier which means CNATRA is challenged to keep a continuous and predictable pilot training schedule.

"A fixed-wing aeroplane designed for aircraft carrier operation has a tail hook and a launch bar. Every single stress that goes through the aeroplane is dwarfed by the stress of launching it from and landing it on a carrier. If a tail hook, a launch bar and associated structural components are required in the UJTS, the aircraft will have to be designed from scratch. There are no existing aeroplanes with those systems fitted. Such a requirement will drive cost, schedule, and risk.

"I cringed when I learned that carriers might be removed from the training, but the more I've talked to the folks in CNATRA, I get it. It does appear that the US Navy is moving away from the aircraft carrier being a firm requirement for those reasons."

Prior to landing aboard a carrier for the first time, nugget pilots perform repetitive touch and go landings on the runway which is marked to replicate the landing area of a carrier's flight deck to simulate landing on an aircraft carrier. Known as 'field carrier landing practice' or FCLP it is required flight training that precedes carrier landing operations and simulates, as near as practicable, the conditions encountered during carrier landing operations.

Discussing the M-346's applicability to the PLM, Steve Helmer, a former US Navy F/A-18 pilot and a demonstration pilot for Textron Aviation Defense said: "One of the strengths of the M-346, is that the aeroplane already has digital fly-by-wire flight controls. That means it can readily be modified to accept PLM control schemes. Using an engineering simulator, provided promising results for equipping the aircraft with PLM for use at the field. That's a developmental path based on the RFI.

"By putting PLM into the aeroplane, we can closely mimic the approach modes the student will use to go to the ship. FCLP Will utilise the same procedures and all the same control schemes which will transfer very positively to a fleet aircraft. On top of that, integration of the simulator and the ground-based training systems, will allow us to simulate going to the ship and get us one step closer to that final product, so when a student flies FCLP and goes to the ship for the first time they will have already flown the procedure in a high-fidelity simulator.

"When the Naval Air Systems Command finally solidifies its RFP, we suspect the precision landing mode, and a large area display will be in the aircraft configuration we offer. And because the aeroplane will be future proofed if you will, with an open architecture concept, the M-346N would be easily modifiable as the training continues to evolve.

"The M-346 IFTS can provide basic and high-level training. At the basic level a nugget pilot can learn to fly a jet and at a higher-level a pilot can use the aeroplane and the live virtual constructive element with multiple aeroplanes involved, and conduct weapons delivery, an air-to-air intercept, or in a more intimate

Below: **A computer-generated image of an M-346N trainer leading a formation of Naval Air Training Command Beechcraft aircraft, left to right, T-44 Pegasus, T-54A METS, M-346N, T-6B Texan and the T-34C Mentor.** Textron Aviation Defense

way, the basic blocking and tackling skills of basic fighter manoeuvres. The most precious thing the M-346N can download to a student who is going to fly the F-35, is an understanding of the communications and the lexicon of flying the aeroplane.

"The M-346 integrated training system can be built into whatever you need it to be with the existing tools, with the built-in ability to adapt the toolset to change the training tactics around the system. A student fresh out of training with the T-6 could attend the IFTS at Deci and with a few minor tweaks could conduct FCLP to easily meet the requirements of the F/A-18, EA-18, and F-35 fleet replacement squadrons.

"Based on the current requirements listed in the RFI, the M-346 advanced jet trainer is the baseline aircraft. Ahead of an RFP being issued, we're already doing some interesting air-to-air training with simulated radar that's informed with a data link. We're also doing some interesting events with GPS-guided weapons. We believe the navy will require a larger cockpit display, which is not part of the current baseline. Other options available are a radar, an EO/IR sensor, and live weapons' carriage.

"One of the M-346N's strengths is modularity which enables the aeroplane's configuration to be changed. So, if the navy wants to drop live training munitions,

M-346 CHARACTERISTICS

Length	11.49m (37.70ft)
Height	4.91m (16.11ft)
Wingspan	9.72m (31.89ft)
Wing area	23.52m^2 (253.2ft^2)
Weight empty	4,900kg (10,803lb)
Max take-off weight	9,600kg (21,165lb)
Max take-off weight trainer	7,400kg (16,310lb)
Max internal fuel weight	2,000kg (4,410lb)
Max external fuel three 630lit tanks	1,515kg (3,340lb)
Max external payload	2,200kg (4,850lb)
Max rate of climb	22,000ft/min (6,705m/min)
Service ceiling	45,000ft (13,716m)
Max operating speed sea level	590kts (1,100kph)
Max operating speed at sea level	572kts (1,050kph)
Stall speed	95kts (176kph)
G limits	+8/-3g
Max sustained load factor at sea level	8g
Max sustained load factor at 15,000ft	5.2g
Max sustained turn rate at 15,000ft	13° per second
Take-off ground run at sea level	1,310ft (400m)
Landing run at sea level with 20% internal fuel	1,800ft (550m)
Range clean	1,070nm (1,980km)
Range with three external tanks	1,470nm (2,720km)
Power Plant	Two Honeywell F124-GA-200s each rated at 6,280lb (27.93kN)

or conduct intercept training with a live radar or advanced air-to-air training with live and synthetic targets we can provide those. With the M-346N, we can tailor training to be more efficient.

"In terms of downloading flight training from the fleet replacement squadrons, the M-346N can train for the use of precision guided munitions, advanced air-to-air engagements, aerial refuelling, NVGs, fly with what looks like a radar on their screen, and information management.

"The system can be adapted for new sensors, new training concepts, and the way students learn as they move through the training command. These factors represent a step change in the way we think about training aviators."

Steve Helmer said concern about information management is valid: "How do we teach data management in a task saturated environment? With the ability to data link simulators, aircraft and ground stations together in a live virtual constructive environment, you can download pretty much whatever mission set you want. For example, a 2 v x self-escort strike. Two friendly aeroplanes flying formation on each other, in a completely constructive environment, simulating a flight into enemy territory to drop precision-guided munitions with an air picture. That's something we would not have done until towards the end of the F/A-18 fleet replacement squadron course. So, the fact that the Italian Air Force is doing that with the equivalent of advanced jet students today, demonstrates the downloading concept very well. I'm confident that whatever syllabus the navy decides to go with, we're going to be able to provide a product that's good at it."

If the Textron-Leonardo team eventually wins the UJTS competition, Tom Webster anticipates the initial few aeroplanes will be built in Venegono, Italy in the interest of speed and starting the EMD phase as soon as possible to shorten its duration. Then the company will transition to a split production between Italy and a final assembly location somewhere in the US.

UNDERGRADUATE JET TRAINING SYSTEM

"Naval Air Systems Command and CNATRA will finish an analysis of alternatives this year. There is a budget allocation in the 2026 timeframe for the first 10 aeroplanes, and for 12 in 2027, 2028, and 2029. Even though we don't have an RFP, we're currently doing things on the navy's behalf, based on what we think we know. So, when the RFP is issued, we think we'll be well postured to give them a really low risk, no drama solution," he concluded.

Italy's Master

The origin of the M-346 Master dates to the partnership that Aermacchi formed with Yakovlev, and the launch of the Yak/AEM-130D, in 1993. Cooperation continued until 1999, when the two companies decided to continue developing the project according to their own ideas. The following year Aermacchi launched the M-346, a trainer aircraft more suited to Western markets and quite different from the Yak-130. The first prototype (c/n P.001) flew for the first time on July 15, 2004, followed by P.002, and the first pre-series production sample (c/n LRIP.00).

Aircraft P.001 was lost in an accident in November 2011, while LRIP.00 was written off in another accident in May 2013; in both cases, the crews ejected safely. Each accident had a different cause due to the different configuration of each prototype. Aermacchi kept its customers constantly informed about the investigations and modifications introduced on the series production aircraft.

To continue with flight test activity, one aircraft built in the first lot for the Aeronautica Militare (serial number MM.55152) was assigned to Alenia Aermacchi, so a new airframe was built for the air force to restore its six-aircraft fleet.

Since late 2010, M-346 assembly has taken place on a new digital base production line at Alenia-Aermacchi's

Left: **Italian Air Force M-346 Master trainer jets.** Leonardo

UNDERGRADUATE JET TRAINING SYSTEM

Left: **A computer-generated image of an M-346N trainer in a light grey colour scheme.** Textron Aviation Defense

Below: **An Italian Air Force M-346N Master jet trainer flying over the Tyrrhenian Sea.** Leonardo

(Leonardo since 2016) Venegono facility capable of building up to four aircraft per month.

Systems of a Master

The M-346 is packed with systems essential for a 21st century jet trainer aircraft: open architecture avionics managed through a dual MIL-STD-1553B digital bus; two (forward and aft) full glass cockpits each with a head-up display and three multi-function displays; an embedded tactical training simulation capability providing air-to-air and air-to-surface training simulation, radar, electronic warfare, data link and armament.

Thanks to cooperation with Israeli company Elbit, the M-346 is also compatible with a multi-function helmet-mounted display that includes virtual HUD, day and night (with NVGs) operations.

Two Honeywell F124 engines which are cheap to operate, reliable, light, and powerful, coupled with the M-346's lightweight and aerodynamically advanced airframe, give the M-346 excellent performance.

The M-346 has an in-flight refuelling capability and in some areas of its flight envelope offers similar performance to

US NAVY AND MARINE CORPS YEARBOOK **2024**

UNDERGRADUATE JET TRAINING SYSTEM

an F-16, with the ability to fly at 30° angle of attack. Aspects that perhaps explain why the M-346 is a capable lead-in-fighter trainer (LIFT) and why some air forces consider the aircraft for the light attack role.

Growth Potential
Alenia-Aermacchi designed the M-346 with growth potential: the air intakes can accept an airflow 20% greater than required by the F124 engine, allowing more powerful engines to be fitted, and the electrical system has a 75% power reserve, so future avionic systems, including a self-defence suite and a radar could be powered.

For any air force with a limited budget the aircraft's ability to carry a 3,100kg (6,828lb) stores payload on five hard points, three of which are wet for 630lit (166 US gal) fuel tanks make it suitable for the light fighter role. The Master can also substitute front line aircraft in the continuation training role, which is an attractive capability for any an air force that needs to save flying hours on its front-line fighters.

Italian Air Force Service
The first contract with the Italian Ministry of Defence was signed in November 2009, covering the first lot of six aircraft (designated T-346As) plus an integrated training system. Lot 1 was divided into two batches: the first batch included two aircraft (first flight on March 31, 2011) destined for the Reparto Sperimentale Volo (Flight Test Wing) based at Pratica di Mare Air Base for operational test and evaluation (OT&E) between March and September 2012. Test results led to modifications, especially software, which required a period of follow-on OT&E in the spring of 2014.

On February 26, 2015, 212° Gruppo, part of 61° Stormo based at Lecce Air Base received the first Aeronautica Militare T-346A, but the type had already operated at Lecce in the summer of 2014 to qualify the first instructors.

Below: Two Italian Air Force M-346 Master jet trainers taxi to the ramp at Lecce Air Base, Italy. Leonardo

UNDERGRADUATE JET TRAINING SYSTEM

A second contract for three aircraft was signed on December 22, 2014, followed by a third on March 21, 2016 covering nine more for delivery between late 2016 and 2018 – a total of 18 T-346As.

The first training course (phase 4) started in August 2015.

Exports

The first international contract was signed with the Republic of Singapore Air Force in September 2010. The M-346 won the Fighter Wing Course programme to find the successor to the A-4S Skyhawk. Construction of the first Singaporean aircraft started in January 2011, and delivery of the first two of 12 aircraft occurred in November 2012 to BA120 Cazaux, France, where the Republic of Singapore Air Force 150 Squadron is based. Deliveries were completed in March 2014.

In July 2012, Israel signed Alenia-Aermacchi's third export contract covering 30 M-346I Lavi (lion cub), logistics, maintenance, and training. The aircraft and an integrated training system are managed by Thor, a joint-venture established by Israel Aircraft Industries and Elbit, to provide training services to the Israel Air and Space Force for 20 years.

Roll-out of the first Israeli aircraft occurred on March 20, 2014. Following completion of an initial training phase for the first cadre of Israeli instructor pilots in Italy, the first two M-346I Lavi were delivered to Hatzerim Air Base in July and assigned to 102 Squadron replacing the unit's A-4 Skyhawks in the LIFT role.

The most recent competition to be won by the M-346 was in February 2014 when Poland signed for eight aircraft, full mission simulators and flight training devices plus logistic support and training. In 2018, the Polish government signed for eight more M-346s, four in March and four in December. Azerbaijan and Greece have also placed orders for the M-346.

Riccardo Niccoli

UNDERGRADUATE JET TRAINING SYSTEM

TF-50N

In response to the US Navy's call for aircraft proposals for their Undergraduate Jet Training System, Lockheed Martin has partnered with Korea Aerospace Industries to offer the TF-50N.

UNDERGRADUATE JET TRAINING SYSTEM

Below:
A computer-generated image of a TF-50N in the orange and white colours currently painted on Naval Air Training Command's T-45 Goshawk.
Lockheed Martin

WHEN NAVAL AIR Systems Command issued a Request for Information (RFI) for the Undergraduate Jet Training System (UJTS), they were looking to replace the current tandem-seat, carrier capable, T-45 Goshawk used for intermediate and advanced jet training. The T-45 is one part of an established training system and Lockheed Martin see their TF-50N jet trainer as the ideal replacement. Mike Kelley, the company's director of campaigns for the integrated fighter group said: "The T-50 is a proven platform. Almost 300 are on order or already delivered across seven different countries, with 300,000 flight hours fleet wide and an aircraft availability rate of 90%.

"Because the T-50 is an advanced jet trainer, it helps reduce the learning curve for the pilots and gets them into the operational aircraft sooner than previous legacy aircraft, especially fifth-generation aircraft like the F-35. The TF-50N is a low-risk solution for the US Navy and Marine Corps requirements. We've been producing the aircraft for a while, and we have developed several variants. We're not only committed to providing the aircraft, but a holistic training system solution that's designed to provide affordability and efficiency in operation, sustainment, and follow-on modernisation. We've got a modular system that will enable rapid, continued modernisation, not just for the requirements that the US Navy is going to be publishing in its UJTS RFP, but also future requirements."

UNDERGRADUATE JET TRAINING SYSTEM

T-50 CHARACTERISTICS

Length	13.1m (43ft 1in)
Height	4.9m (16ft 2in)
Wingspan	9.1m (29ft 10in)
Wing area	23.7m^2 (255.0ft^2)
Weight empty	6,480kg (14,285lb)
Max TO weight	9,300kg (20,589lb) [clean] 12,400kg (27,300lb) [with external stores]
Max fuel weight	2,200kg (4,895lb) [internal]
Max stores payload	4,750kg (10,500lb) [external]
Max rate of climb	39,600ft/min (12,000m/min)
Time to height	two minutes to 30,000ft (9,145m)
Absolute ceiling	55,000ft (16,765m)
Service ceiling	49,000ft (14,935m)
Max operating speed	815kts
Max operating Mach	1.5 [design] 1.3 [tested]
Stall speed	105kts
G limits	+8/-3
Range	1,403nm with three 150 US gal drop tanks
Service structural life (design)	10,000 hours (8,300 hours for TA-50 and FA-50)
Data	Lockheed Martin

Detailing the holistic training solution, Mike Kelley said: "It's a solution that deals with all aspects of the training experience. It includes the TF-50N aircraft itself with embedded synthetic training on board; there's similar technology in the immersive ground-based training system for maintenance personnel who can utilise virtual reality techniques; cockpit simulators; and a training management system which manages the courseware, the students, and the training they've received throughout the course."

According to Lockheed Martin, the TF-50N optimises training by allowing students to focus their airmanship skills on improved aero performance, digital flight controls, and next-generation sensor systems. The platform has significantly reduced required flight training hours for frontline aircraft.

Mike Kelley continued: "Once the US Navy issues an RFP, we'll know the full range of requirements and will adapt the design and the systems to meet those requirements as needed. We already know the things that will differ between a land-based T-50 and a marinized TF-50N.

"Naval Air Systems Command and the Chief of Naval Air Training [CNATRA] are likely to have either a field carrier landing practice [FCLP] requirement, or potentially a carrier capable requirement. The latter will require a higher sink rate capability, more shock and vibration requirements, strengthened landing gear, a strengthened airframe, a launch bar and a tailhook which would require some redesign.

"The aircraft's handling qualities [around an aircraft carrier] will be straightforward to incorporate because the T-50 is a digital aircraft, but we will need to include all the aspects that help pilots train to land the aeroplane in a simulated or real way on the carrier."

Providing more details, Jim Mlynarski, Lockheed Martin's TF-50N capture manager said: "We're working with our partners at Korea Aerospace Industries [KAI], to look at what upgrades will be needed, what systems need to be changed, which ones are already good enough. With each new customer that procures the T-50 more systems are integrated on the aircraft which puts the jet closer to what we expect of the US Navy's requirements."

Without a definitive set of requirements, Lockheed Martin and KAI are working with their supply base to determine what might have to be done to establish what options are on the table when the requirement is issued. Naval Air Systems Command and CNATRA is potentially changing from a carrier qualification to FCLP qualification. "The requirements we've seen in the last few RFIs provide an understanding of the different paths we may have to go down with our supply base."

Discussing the ability of the TF-50N training system to get nugget pilots to fleet replacement squadrons more quickly and with more capability so CNATRA can look at the syllabus and improve on what they currently provide with the T-45 Goshawk, Mike Kelley said: "One of the big advances that's been made over the last 20 years is the evolution of synthetic training. Legacy training aircraft weren't designed with that in mind, but the ability to simulate different

UNDERGRADUATE JET TRAINING SYSTEM

Above: **A Republic of Korea Air Force TA-50 inside a hardened aircraft shelter.** Korea Aerospace Industries

Below left: **Head-on view of a TF-50N.** Lockheed Martin

sensors and environments and have a virtual wingman in the cockpit allows you to conduct more thorough training activities and consequently enables better outcomes for the pilots."

"We've been working with Red 6, a company that develops augmented reality. We've integrated their technology into our cockpit demonstrator system to prove the concept and see the benefit. Red 6 has developed the Airborn, Tactical Augmented Reality System or ATARS. The objective is to put that technology into a visor like a helmet-mounted display and be able to fly with a virtual wingman to conduct mission sets without having to fly with an actual airborne wingman. So, there's a cost saving per flying hour with the ability to complete different missions on the same sortie to give the student pilot a more realistic and thorough training experience at a lower cost."

Augmented Reality

On February 12, 2024, Lockheed Martin and Red 6 announced an effort to integrate the latest Red 6 augmented reality (AR) training technology with a TF-50 simulator. This phase-one milestone will facilitate broader evaluation of AR applications and accelerate their integration into the TF-50 aircraft design, in support of increasing pilot readiness with the least amount of flight hours.

According to Daniel Robinson, founder and CEO of Red 6: "ATARS is the technology that for the first time ever, enables a complete live virtual and constructive ecosystem in the airborne environment, from beyond visual range to within visual range."

Mike Kelley said that if the Lockheed Martin-KAI team eventually wins the UJTS competition: "Our expectation is that we would have a final assembly and checkout facility [FACO] here in the US, likely located at our facility in Greenville, South Carolina. We envision that KAI would build some of the major components [likely the wing, fuselage, and tail sections] in the Republic of Korea and ship them to the States for final assembly at the FACO, but at the time we'll have to determine what the most

UNDERGRADUATE JET TRAINING SYSTEM

cost effective and high-quality way to do the assembly process would be."

Providing additional context on the award timing, Jim Mlynarski said: "We understand the UJTS programme is currently undergoing its analysis of alternatives, so there are still decisions to be made. The last RFI was issued on June 26 [2024]. A RFP might be issued, with a targeted award currently expected in FY2028."

T-50 Golden Eagle

The Korea Aerospace Industry-Lockheed Martin T-50 Golden Eagle series of advanced trainers and lightweight fighters exemplifies the increasing capability of the Republic of Korea (RoK) aerospace industry. The first RoK aircraft to be exported, it was also a stepping stone to designing, developing, and producing the indigenous fifth-generation KF-21 Boramae fighter aircraft.

The design's high performance, low cost ($18-40m per aircraft depending on version and quantity) and quality of fabrication have secured multiple export customers.

From Design to Operational Flying

The T-50 series was intended to replace Republic of Korea Air Force (RoKAF) Northrop T-38s and F-5s in the training role, providing a lead-in for conversion to the next generation of fighters. Weapons delivery capability for training (while retaining an operational role) would be handled by an armed trainer version.

Lockheed Martin's involvement with the Korean aerospace industry increased with the KF-16 fighter procurement programme in the 1980s. The new trainer design was a spin-off from the KF-16 design and fabrication investment, giving it a high-performance combat-aircraft origin. Lockheed Martin's offset package included their participation in the new programme, starting with the initial design which was completed by 1995. Development started in 1997, with the RoK government providing 70% of the funding, 17% from Samsung Aerospace (merged into KAI in 1999) and the remaining 13% from Lockheed Martin.

Above: **Plan view of a TF-50N.**
Lockheed Martin

Below: **Side-on view of Republic of Korea Air Force TA-50 12-079.**
Korea Aerospace Industries

UNDERGRADUATE JET TRAINING SYSTEM

The T-50 trainer and the A-50 light fighter – as they were re-designated in 2000 – were developed together, producing two flying prototypes of each (plus two non-flying ground and static test airframes). The first prototype was rolled out in October 2001, the first flight took place in August 2002 and by February 2003, supersonic flight had been achieved.

Following the RoKAF's initial order for 25 T-50s, production started in December 2003 at KAI's Sacheon facility. The first deliveries took place in December 2005. After receiving 12 T-50s, 203rd Squadron at Gwangju Air Base started training operations in March 2007.

T-50 follow-on orders brought total deliveries of the basic version – unarmed and without a radar – up to 50. Deliveries were completed by 2011, equipping the 189th and 203rd Training Squadrons at Gwangju and the 281st Test and Evaluation Squadron at Sacheon.

Above: **The level of the seats in the forward and aft cockpits of the TA-50 will afford the student and instructor pilot clear visibility.**
Korea Aerospace Industries

The ten T-50B versions for the RoKAF's Black Eagles formation air display team were modified T-50s with specialised equipment including oil tanks for making coloured smoke. They were ordered in 2008 under a KRW220bn ($185m) contract and were delivered to the team in 2009.

Systems

In addition to its supersonic maximum speed and fighter-like manoeuvrability, the T-50 incorporates systems intended to facilitate trainees' transition to flying

UNDERGRADUATE JET TRAINING SYSTEM

fourth and fifth generation fighters. From the engine to the cockpit, the T-50 series uses the same systems currently operational on US and other Western combat aircraft.

The T-50 series is powered by a General Electric F404-GE-102 turbofan (17,700lb/78.7kN thrust with afterburning), equipped with full authority digital engine control. The engine is produced under license by Hanhwa (formerly Samsung) Techwin, a GE industrial partner since the 1980s.

Advanced pilot trainees fly the T-50. Initial training is on the KAI K-1 Wonngbi turboprop. Trainees then transition to pure jets on the KAI KT-100 basic trainer and then to the T-50.

Indonesia was the first export customer, ordering 16 T-50Is – based on the TA-50 – in April 2011, as part of an agreement to increase access to each other's markets and enhance cooperation between aerospace industries. Deliveries started in September 2013 and were completed in 2014. The T-50Is serve with 15th Squadron at Iswahyundi Air Base in east Java, where they provide a 90 flight-

UNDERGRADUATE JET TRAINING SYSTEM

Left: Republic of Korea Air Force TA-50 12-079 approaches the runway.
Korea Aerospace Industries

Below: The TA-50 fuselage measures 43ft 1in in length, 4ft 3in longer than the current T-45 Goshawk trainer.
Korea Aerospace Industries

hour lead-in training course for pilots transitioning to fighters.

KAI supplied another six T-50s to Indonesia following a contract announcement in July 2021.

Iraq ordered 24 T-50IQ versions in 2013 as part of a $1.1bn package including pilot training, technical support, and air base upgrades. Intended for training and light attack, the T-50IQ reportedly has the same combat capability as the FA-50. The first five were delivered in 2015 to the Iraqis in the RoK, where they carried out pilot training. T-50IQ aircraft equip the 204th Squadron at Al Sahra/Tikrit Air Base.

Thailand's $110m order for four T-50THs – based on the TA-50 – plus options for a further 20 was announced in September 2015. Intended as an L-39 replacement, the T-50TH was selected over strong competition which included the Italian Alenia Aermacchi M-346, Chinese Hongdu L-15, and the Textron AirLand Scorpion. Thailand's government approved the procurement of eight more T-50TH aircraft in July 2017. **David C Isby**

MULTI-SERVICE PILOT TRAINING SYSTEM

T-44 PEGASUS

The Beechcraft C90-based T-44 Pegasus aircraft is the US Navy's only multi-engine advanced pilot training aircraft. Two squadrons fly the T-44 from NAS Corpus Christi in Texas. Its days are now numbered, so we took the opportunity to cover the aircraft before its sundown.

TRAINING AIR WING 4 receives about 430 naval flight students per year from a myriad of different communities: US Navy, US Marine Corps, the US Coast Guard, as well as international students. All multi-engine naval flight students from whichever service start their primary flight training in the T-6 with either VT-27 or VT-28 based at Naval Air Station Corpus Christi, Texas or with one of the three T-6 squadrons based at Naval Air Station Whiting Field, Florida. About 40% of all the flight students go through primary training with TAW-4. Students selected for the C-130, E-2, E-6, P-8, or V-22 complete their advanced multi engine flight training with either VT-31 or VT-35 at Corpus Christi.

Course Details

The mission of advanced multi-engine multi-service pilot training system (MPTS) is to develop proficiency in multi-engine flight,

MULTI-SERVICE PILOT TRAINING SYSTEM

advanced instruments, crew resource management/pilot-in-command proficiency, and track-specific tactics. At the successful completion of this phase of aviation training, the flight student will be designated a naval aviator qualified in multi-engine aircraft and will have earned a standard instrument rating.

Prerequisite training for fixed-wing candidates is successful completion of T-6B primary pilot training, and for tiltrotor candidates, successful completion of the intermediate tiltrotor helicopter MPTS curriculum.

T-44C advanced multi-engine MPTS consists of multi-engine training for US Navy, US Marine Corps, US Coast Guard, and international NFSs who will go to multi-engine follow-on pipelines.

Each phase is divided into stages. Stages are grouped by like flight training regimes: contact, instrument, navigation, formation, and tactical. Each stage is subdivided into training blocks. The training blocks consist of a specified number of flights. Manoeuvre item files identify the acceptable level of performance that must be achieved at the completion of each training block.

Progression through the syllabus requires the naval flight student (NFS) to fly syllabus events within each stage sequentially. An NFS cannot start a block without all prerequisites. NFSs

FIRST NAVY OSPREY PILOT GRADUATES

The US Navy's first new accession CMV-22B Osprey pilot graduated from flight school after earning his naval aviator designation at Naval Air Station Corpus Christi on December 6, 2019.

Lieutenant Caleb Nicholson completed primary flight training with VT-28 'Rangers' at NAS Corpus Christi, after which he reported to HT-18 'Vigilant Eagles' at NAS Whiting Field, Florida for intermediate helicopter training. He then reported to TAW-4 and subsequently to VT-35 'Stingrays' for advanced training.

VT-35 and VT-31 are the only two advanced training squadrons for multi-engine aircraft, however VT-35 is the only squadron to train future V-22 Osprey pilots. Student naval aviators fly the T-44C Pegasus, a twin-engine, pressurised, fixed-wing monoplane.

The training syllabus, which is the same for both navy and marine corps pilots, focuses on advanced contact and instrument flight, formation flying, overwater navigation, and low-level tactical formation flying with a heavy focus on crew Resource Management and automated flight.

VT-35 executes more than 14,000 flight hours each year, encompassing more than 52,000 landings and nearly 9,500 student flight-training events. Graduates report for subsequent training at their respective fleet replacement squadron according to their selected platform.

Lt Nicholson subsequently began the Osprey training curriculum with Marine Medium Lift Tiltrotor Squadron 204 (VMMT-204) at Marine Corps Air Station New River, North Carolina. Upon successful completion, he joined Fleet Logistics Multi-Mission Squadron 30 (VRM-30) 'Titans' based at NAS North Island in San Diego equipped with the CMV-22B tasked with the carrier onboard delivery (COD) mission.

VRM-30 stood up December 14, 2018, and reports to Fleet Logistics Multi-Mission Wing at North Island.

Training Air Wing 4 is one of five wings under Chief of Naval Air Training (CNATRA) headquartered in Corpus Christi.

Below: **T-44 Pegasus aircraft parked on the Naval Air Station Corpus Christi flightline. Maritime and advanced tilt-rotor training is conducted in the T-44 at Training Squadron 31 and 35 (VT-31 and VT-35) in Training Air Wing Four. The T-44C will begin sundown in late October, 2024, six months after the first delivery of the T-54A.** US Navy/Richard Stewart

MULTI-SERVICE PILOT TRAINING SYSTEM

may be in different stages or blocks simultaneously. Where applicable, NFSs will be eligible for, and prepared for, more than one syllabus event. System training management is designed to facilitate two graded events (flight, simulator, or exam) per NFS, per day.

Student naval aviators (SNAs) with previous flight experience or who have demonstrated exceptional proficiency may warrant accelerated progression, also known as proficiency advance. A squadron CO can advance, and is encouraged to advance, an SNA to the next block of instruction when all required items for the current block of instruction meet or exceed performance prerequisites for the follow-on block of training. It's laid down that the policy should not be used to meet squadron production goals; it is strictly for instances where demonstrated proficiency makes completion of all events within a block of instruction unnecessary.

The squadron closely monitors the progress of accelerated SNAs and if their performance suffers due to acceleration, they can be returned to normal syllabus progression. Another requirement is for NFSs to accomplish previously introduced manoeuvres frequently enough to

Above: Instructor pilots assigned to Training Squadron 31 (VT-31) 'Wise Owls' based at Naval Air Station Corpus Christi conduct a formation flight in T-44C Pegasus aircraft. VT-31 conducts intermediate and advanced multi-engine flight training for the navy, marine corps, coast guard and select international military partners.
US Navy/Lt Michelle Tucker

Left: US Navy/Lt Michelle Tucker

MULTI-SERVICE PILOT TRAINING SYSTEM

Above: **An instructor pilot assigned to Training Squadron 31 (VT-31) 'Wise Owls' conducts a pre-flight inspection on a T-44C Pegasus at Naval Air Station Corpus Christi, Texas.** US Navy/Lt Michelle Tucker

ensure that their required proficiency is maintained.

Instructors are required to plan and execute student missions to meet Hours/X (H/X) as closely as possible. If an actual sortie length varies from the required standard by more than 0.3 hours (either more or less), the instructor has to note why.

Special syllabus requirements (SSRs) are allocated to blocks. And, unless noted otherwise, instructor pilots (Ips) can accomplish their SSRs on any flight within the block. However, they all need to be completed in the specified block.

Additionally, the class advisor conducts weekly aviation training jacket reviews in accordance with the Naval Air Training Class Advisor Program and the training forms are reviewed before each flight or simulator event.

Left: **An instructor pilot and a student naval aviator assigned to Training Squadron 31 (VT-31) 'Wise Owls' based at Naval Air Station Corpus Christi, Texas, taxi out for a training flight in a T-44C Pegasus aircraft.** US Navy/Lt Michelle Tucker

US NAVY AND MARINE CORPS YEARBOOK 2024

MULTI-SERVICE PILOT TRAINING SYSTEM

Left: **A T-44C Pegasus aircraft assigned to Training Air Wing 4 (TAW-4) sits on the flight line at Naval Air Station Corpus Christi, Texas.** US Navy/Lt Michelle Tucker

Below left: **An instructor pilot assigned to Training Squadron 31 (VT-31) 'Wise Owls' based at Naval Air Station Corpus Christ, Texas, reviews a chart during a formation flight brief.** US Navy/Lt Michelle Tucker

MULTI-SERVICE PILOT TRAINING SYSTEM

T-44 CHARACTERISTICS

Length	35ft 6in (10.82m)
Height	14ft 3in (4.34m)
Wingspan	50ft 3in (15.32m)
Weight empty	6,246lb (2,833kg)
Max take-off weight	9,650lb (4,377kg)
Max airspeed	245kts
Service ceiling	31,300ft
Max range	1,300nm
Crew	instructor pilot, two student pilots

T-44 Sundown

Over the next two years, CNATRA is replacing 55 T-44 Pegasus aircraft with 64 T-54s, and six T-44 simulators with eight T-54 simulators and desktop trainer systems. Discussing the transition, Lieutenant Commander Enriquez, multi-engine acquisition officer for CNATRA said: "We should receive our final T-54 aircraft by the beginning of 2026. The eight new simulators will all be government owned, and government operated, for the T-54. Use of virtual reality [VR] and augmented reality may come into play in the future, but those of us who were part of the planning didn't think it was needed, since a lot of multi engine flying involves multi-pilot operation where the pilots need to speak with one another, so having a VR headset on might not be optimal training when they're trying to work with their co-pilot.

"We receive 430 students per year between VT-31 and VT-35 which requires approximately 33,000 flight hours a year for multi engine training, so each student graduates with about 76 to 80 flight hours. They also get an equivalent amount of time in the simulators.

"TAW-4 operates with contractor maintenance. Currently we're on the interim maintenance contract while we acquire the new aircraft, but after a year or so, there will be a long-term T-54 maintenance contract with a civilian company."

Below: **The T-44's conversion from the T-44A to the T-44C introduced an avionics upgrade to include the cockpit's multi-function displays.**
US Navy/Richard Stewart

MULTI-ENGINE TRAINING SYSTEM

T-54A
MULTI-ENGINE TRAINER

Textron Aviation Defense won a contract to supply US Naval Training Command with King Air 260 aircraft for the Multi-Engine Training System programme.

MULTI-ENGINE TRAINING SYSTEM

CAPTAIN LINDEN WHITMER is the programme executive officer for PMA-273, Naval Air Systems Command's management authority for all the aircraft, almost 700 of them, operated by Naval Training Command (CNATRA).

One of the recapitalisation programmes currently on his watch is the Multi-Engine Training System which is replacing the Beech T-44 Pegasus operated by Training Air Wing 4 (TAW-4) based at Naval Air Station Corpus Christi, Texas with a derivative of the Beechcraft King Air 260, designated the T-54A by the US Navy.

According to a navy press release: "On January 25, 2024, Naval Air Systems Command awarded Textron Aviation a single, firm-fixed-price contract to develop the T-54A multi-engine training system (METS) aircraft. The T-54A will provide advanced instrument and asymmetric engine handling training to student naval aviators selected for multi-engine fleet communities.

Captain Holly Shoger, then PMA-273's programme manager said: "The T-54A will include the latest avionics and navigational updates, such as virtual reality and augmented reality devices, to ensure pilots are ready to face any challenges that come their way in tomorrow's battlespace.

"The base contract is valued at $113.1 million for ten aircraft. The total contract value, including the base and contract options, is $677.2 million for the procurement of up to 64 aircraft. The contract also covers support equipment, spares, and initial training. The aircraft deliveries are scheduled from calendar year 2024 to 2026.

"The T-54A aircraft features a pressurised aircraft cockpit with side-by-side seating, a jump seat, and a reconfigurable cargo bay in the cabin. The aircraft has more range than a T-44, so it can fly for longer and accomplish more training per sortie.

"The cockpit is equipped with the Collins Aerospace Pro Line Fusion avionics suite; three 14in multifunction displays with a digital moving map; auto-throttle system; multi-scan weather radar; dual flight management system; redundant ultra-high frequency and very high frequency radios; an integrated global positioning system/inertial navigation system; automatic dependent surveillance-broadcast; radar altimeter; integrated terrain awareness and warning system; traffic alert and collision avoidance; engine indicating and crew alerting system; and a cockpit data recorder.

"Using a skills-based approach to training with just-in-time methodology, the T-54A is designed to enhance multi-engine training opportunities to an extent that fleet replacement squadrons can spend less time on foundational skills and focus more on mission requirements.

Below: **A computer-generated image of a T-54A.** Commander, Naval Air Training Command

MULTI-ENGINE TRAINING SYSTEM

"Additionally, the aircraft's technology will capture data that allows for conditioned-based maintenance plus, a capability that enables the navy to trend aircraft health over time to facilitate improved maintenance planning and efficiency."

Explaining, Captain Whitmer said: "The T-54's digital cockpit and flight management system will best prepare navy, marine corps, and coast guard student pilots heading to fleet-assigned C-130 Hercules, E-2 Hawkeye, P-8 Poseidon, V-22 Osprey and HC-144 squadrons, aircraft equipped with digital cockpits and upgraded flight management systems.

"Textron Aviation Defense delivered the first T-54A aircraft to TAW-4 in April and had delivered the first ten aircraft by the end of August. TAW-4 completed its safe-for-flight certification in July and is now training instructors pilots on the aircraft and preparing them to start training the first student pilots in Q1 2025.

"Because the T-54 is a derivative of the commercial King Air 260 aeroplane and did not undergo any significant changes, the decision was made to not conduct any major development or operational flight testing. Instructor pilots who are currently flying the T-54 report any issues they discover with the aircraft to CNATRA, PMA-273 and Textron, who, in the event, work together to remedy the problem.

"We have incorporated an angle-of-attack indexer, a device that E-2 Hawkeye pilots use to land onboard aircraft carriers, at a similar place to the flight deck of an E-2 aircraft. We worked with CNATRA to ensure the cockpit meets the requirements for an angle-of-attack indexer. We also installed a UHF radio and identification devices that make the aircraft compliant to operate in airspace used by TAW-4."

Another major component of the METS is the ground-based training system. In February 2024, a firm-fixed-price contract valued at $54.8m was award to TRU Simulation Plus Training based in Lutz, Florida. The contract includes five T-54A operational flight trainers, three unit training devices, 21 desktop avionics trainers, eight brief/debrief systems and one software support station including associated logistical support, and instructor, operator, and maintenance training. Deliveries are planned to begin in December, 2024.

Summing up the programme as of July 2024, Capt Whitmer said: "From an execution standpoint, we're delivering airplanes and we're on track to meet initial operating capability, to meet the needs of CNATRA for training the next generation of pilots."

Right: **The T-54A aircraft is powered by two Pratt & Whitney Canada PT6A-52 turboprop engines each rated at 850shp with Hartzell four-blade, composite, constant speed, auto feather propellers.**
Mark Ayton

Below: **T-54A BuNo 170753/G taxies back to parking following a functional check flight at Beech Factory Airport.**
Mark Ayton

MULTI-ENGINE TRAINING SYSTEM

Below: **The US Navy T-54A aircraft is based on the King Air 260 model.**
Mark Ayton

Training Air Wing 4

Lieutenant Commander Mike Enriquez currently serves as the multi-engine acquisition requirements officer for CNATRA, a role he has undertaken since the time of the METS contract award. Prior to this role, Lt Cdr Enriquez served as an instructor pilot on the T-6B Texan and since 2020, the T-44C Pegasus.

Between contract award and receiving the first two aircraft, Lt Cdr Enriquez, and his colleagues at CNATRA wrote the T-54 flight manuals and developed the flight procedures to be used for teaching student pilots. Explaining, Enriquez said: "This involved flight testing with Textron to determine whether the aircraft's systems and devices worked adequately for teaching students. The team also worked with engineers working for TRU Simulation based in Tampa, Florida to develop the T-54 simulators, procedures, and simulated malfunctions in the simulator."

TAW-4 receives about 430 students per year from a myriad of US Navy, US Marine Corps, US Coast Guard, and international communities.

"All multi-engine students from whichever service start with primary flight training in the T-6 with either VT-27 or VT-28 here at Corpus Christi or with one of the three T-6 squadrons based at Naval Air Station Whiting Field, Florida. About 40% of all the flight students come through primary training with TAW-4. Students selected for the C-130, E-2, E-6, P-8, or V-22 complete their advanced multi engine flight training with either VT-31 or VT-35 here at Corpus Christi.

"Adjusting the existing curriculum used with the T-44 to a new curriculum for the T-54 proved a challenge, primarily to accommodate the huge increase in technology and avionics installed in the T-54."

Explaining, Lt Cdr Enriquez said: "The T-44 has flight automation, autopilot, and GPS navigation, but is a much more rudimentary system that teaches students the basics before they fly with more modern avionics with the fleet replacement squadron. The T-54 is equipped with avionics that are more advanced than a lot of the fleet aircraft that our students will go to once they get their wings.

"The T-54 is equipped with an advanced GPS system, an advanced auto pilot system and an auto throttle system, which controls the power levers for you. These systems improve flight safety, but also require more planning to make sure everything functions correctly while you're flying.

"We can't introduce all the modern avionics to the students right away, that would be too much of a change to the cockpit of a T-6, their first aircraft flown in their training. Consequently, we plan to have our student crawl before they walk before they run. We may start teaching students this winter.

"The initial cadre of T-54 pilots assigned to TAW-4 are flying as instructor pilots to figure out what works and what doesn't work. It will be interesting to see how much of the automated systems we can introduce students to right away.

"One benefit of the T-54 is its speed, altitude, and range which means we aren't restrained to the south Texas region to conduct our flight training. We will expand the area that we fly to for instrument flying out to many different places including, Arkansas, Louisiana, North Texas, and Oklahoma. We plan to fly two students and an instructor pilot from NAS Corpus Christi to challenging airfields and airspaces to complete instrument approach procedures, contact landing patterns, and instrument/visual navigation in a hybrid visual and instrument flight rules environment.

MULTI-ENGINE TRAINING SYSTEM

"A typical training flight event encompasses one instructor pilot and two flight students. It requires two and a half hours of flight briefing and pre-flight inspections, four hours of flight training time [with each student flying for two of those hours], and one and a half hours of flight debriefing, postflight inspections, and event grading."

"Given the cabin size and fuel payload, the T-54 provides us the ability to transport other military personnel to other stations while we're flying certain curriculum sorties that are not in-depth, and we are cleared to do. The T-54 is fitted with a different type of seat behind the two pilots' seats compared to the T-44 so that the second student can be more engaged with the flight.

"One additional system fitted is an angle-of-attack or AOA system to support the training of students destined for the E-2 Hawkeye, so they can fly the landing pattern in a different way. Instead of looking at the rate of descent or air speed, you look at the angle-of-attack gauge which judges the profile of your aircraft going through the air, which is what pilots use to land on an aircraft carrier. Students will be able to look at the gauge while they're flying. Procedures for this envelope of flight are still being developed.

MULTI-ENGINE TRAINING SYSTEM

Left: T-54A BuNo 170752/G parked on the flight line at Beech Factory Airport prior to its ferry fight to Naval Air Station Corpus Christi, Texas, and acceptance into Training Air Wing 4's fleet. Mark Ayton

T-54A CHARACTERISTICS

Length	43ft 10in
Height	14ft 10in
Wingspan	57ft 11in
Max take-off weight	12,500lb
Max operating airspeed	259kts
Service ceiling	35,000ft
Mission range	1,640nm
Propulsion	Two Pratt & Whitney Canada PT6A-52 engines
Crew	pilot and student co-pilot

"Each T-54 aircraft cabin will be fitted with three seats, but as many as seven is possible, a running toilet, and the ability to retrofit the cabin into an executive style aircraft, should that need ever arise."

T-54 METS Curriculum

Students start the multi-engine course with about three-weeks of ground school taught by an instructor. They then start training with desktop avionics trainers, a system that simulates the avionics in the cockpit to learn how the various systems work together. Then they start

Right: T-54A BuNo 170746/G parked on the Naval Air Station Corpus Christi flight line. Commander, Naval Air Training Command

Below: T-54A BuNo 170752/G on take-off from Beech Factory Airport on its ferry flight to Naval Air Station Corpus Christi, Texas. Mark Ayton

US NAVY AND MARINE CORPS YEARBOOK 2024

MULTI-ENGINE TRAINING SYSTEM

using a unit training device or a UTD which is the shell of a T-54 aircraft with a functional cockpit surrounded by TV screens used for visual cues. Then they start using a flying training device or an FTD, which is an enclosed simulator system, it's like a bubble surrounding the cockpit which offers a more immersive environment. Each student completes many FTD sessions with an instructor. Then they start flying. For each of the two phases, they complete simulator sessions and then fly, jumping back and forth to introduce new things to them in the simulator before they try it out in the aircraft.

"The course encompasses two phases. Students will fly on instruments and visually during every flight. The first phase will involve normal procedures in the instrument and visual/contact environments. The second phase will incorporate emergency procedures and malfunctions in the instrument and visual/contact environments. Each phase comprises roughly the same number of flights or training events. Each phase comprises roughly the same number of flights or events."

According to Lt Cdr Enriquez, CNATRA plans to allocate the same number of flight hours per student on the T-54, with one difference: the student may not spend as much time in a landing pattern situation or in a non IFR training environment as they would have done in the T-44. Explaining, Lt Cdr Enriquez said: "Because the fleet's multi-engine flying has changed as aircraft avionics have changed, the dynamics of low altitude contact VFR flying isn't emphasised as much as instrument flying, so we might do more instrument flying but in the same number of hours.

"It's a possibility that the T-54 will enable some training to be downloaded from the fleet replacement squadrons. Patrol Squadron 30 (VP-30), the P-8 Poseidon FRS based at Naval Air Station Jacksonville, Florida is looking forward

Above: **The King Air 260-based T-54A has a wingspan of 57ft 11in and a fuselage length of 43ft 10in.** Mark Ayton

to its future students arriving for the course who are already familiar with auto throttles, advanced GPS, and auto pilot, Consequently, VP-30 students won't have to spend so much time learning those skills flying the more costly-to-operate P-8. Our whole ethos is to try to simulate what the students will be experiencing in the fleet while they're here at TAW-4 and train them so they can fly a modern fleet aircraft more easily."

Reflections on the Transition

Commenting on the objectives of the METS, Lt Cdr Enriquez said: "Students don't need to be super proficient at flying the T-54 aircraft. We want to make them proficient in instrument/IFR flying and proficient with crew resource management.

"Students complete top-off phases of training, depending on which platform they will go on to fly once get their

Left: **View of the right wing and winglet of a T-54A aircraft from the main cabin.** Commander, Naval Air Training Command

wings. At that point they have their instrument rating, and start doing maritime formation, aerial refuelling, coast guard pilots do search and rescue, marine corps pilots do low-level tactical formation navigation, navy maritime patrol pilots do over water navigation. These are all short top-off phases which are considered a preparation for the fleet replacement squadron.

"Depending on how the initial training of students and new instructors goes over the next year, determining how things might work better, the transition from simulators to aircraft isn't going to change a whole lot between the T-44 the T-54.

"At TAW-4, Training Squadron 35 will be the first squadron to transition from the T-44C to the T-54A. That will occur between March 2025 and March 2026. Beginning in March 2026, VT-31 will begin ITS transition. The complete transition from the T-44 is set to occur by March 2027."

Right: **In keeping with all aircraft assigned to Training Air Wing 4, T-54A aircraft carry the wing's G tail code.**
Commander, Naval Air Training Command

F/A-18 SUPER HORNET

Above: **An F/A-18E Super Hornet assigned to Strike Fighter Squadron 211 (VFA-211) 'Fighting Checkmates' launches off the flight deck of the Nimitz-class aircraft carrier USS *Theodore Roosevelt* (CVN 71) underway in the US 5th Fleet area of operations.**
US Navy

KEEPING THE

THE F/A-18 SUPER Hornet will remain the numerically predominant aircraft in US Navy carrier air wings into the mid-2030s and will continue to provide significant combat capability into the 2040s. Both postures will be maintained by the Block 3 version, already proven in theatre, it will remain tactically relevant for at least two more decades.

Naval Air Systems Command's PMA-265 manages the Super Hornet weapon system. The organisation often works to short timelines. Within a few days of receiving a request from the fleet it provided an update to the AIM-9X Sidewinder air-to-air missiles, and added additional stores capability on stations 2 and 10, the outer underwing pylons, to enable the four Block 2-equipped Super Hornet squadrons assigned to CVW-3 (VFA-32, VFA-83, VFA-105, VFA-131) embarked aboard the USS *Dwight D Eisenhower* (CVN-69) underway in the Red Sea fighting the Houthis.

PMA-265 continues to ensure that the Super Hornet maintains its tactical relevance, lethality, and sustainability, and will do so for as long as it's needed to be the backbone of US naval carrier aviation.

Discussing current Super Hornet test programmes, Davide Howe, Level 1 IPT lead for the Super Hornet with PMA-265 said: "We're in the developmental phase of ADVEW, the advanced electronic warfare system that will replace the aging original electronic warfare system. We're partnered with PMA-272 and have done much of the integration in house."

The ADVEW system is being developed through a competitive acquisition approach

F/A-18 SUPER HORNET

STING ALIVE

After 26 years in US Navy fleet service, Naval Air Systems Command continues to develop and support the F/A-18 Super Hornet, now operating in Block 3 configuration.

with two companies. According to L3Harris, one of the companies developing ADVEW: "The system is designed to provide F/A-18 jets with state-of-the-art countermeasures to complete missions in an environment where threats and adversaries are becoming more sophisticated.

"ADVEW quickly identifies, prioritises, and defeats threats using advanced self-protection technologies. ADVEW is an integrated electronic support measure/electronic attack system that integrates cutting edge technologies for advanced capability across the full radio frequency (RF) spectrum. Enhanced detection and onboard jamming capabilities protect the F/A-18 aircrew against advanced and emerging RF threats, and it is designed to counter them with advanced electronic countermeasure (ECM) techniques, increasing the survivability of the aircraft and aircrew.

"To provide future maintainability and upgradability, ADVEW uses a modular open systems approach, allowing the insertion of new and upgraded technology, maximising cost-effectiveness and improving speed-to fleet. The system maintains all existing data, mechanical and electrical interfaces for day-one plug-and-play integration onto the platform."

L3Harris produces the ALQ-214 IDECM onboard jammer, a radio frequency (RF) integrated countermeasure system. The (V)3 version currently provides self-protection on US Navy F/A-18 Super Hornet aircraft. The A(V)4 version will replace the (V)3 version and provide enhanced capability in a smaller and lighter form. Additionally, the A(V)4 version can be upgraded with an open system architecture for technology insertion and

US NAVY AND MARINE CORPS YEARBOOK **2024**

F/A-18 SUPER HORNET

EW suite capability pgrades, enabling air superiority against ever-evolving threats.

According to the company: "The IDECM ALQ-214 OBJ features autonomous operations within hostile environments to protect aircrew and aircraft against advanced radio frequency (RF) threats. This protection enables enhanced survivability by allowing the aircrew to concentrate on their mission. The system is designed to counter RF guided threats with proven electronic countermeasures techniques that deny, disrupt, delay, and degrade launch and engagement sequences. Each threat is identified, prioritised, countered, and displayed to the aircrew for situational awareness as well as self-protection. The IDECM ALQ-214 utilises a modular and reprogrammable system to provide theatre specific configurations."

OFP H, OFP CD

Discussing operational flight program (OFP) software configuration sets Davide Howe said that OFPs are no longer designated as H-series anymore. H-series OFPs have been replaced by the continuous integration, delivery, and deployment or CID and D series. "We've transitioned to an agile software build process which enables capability to get out to the fleet more rapidly. If we find a problem, we can quickly address it, test it, and quickly send the fix back to the fleet."

Howe said: "We slowly transitioned out of the H-build process and into the agile CIDD process. Operational test has been integrated into the agile software development so the fleet can receive software builds early in the development cycle, they can identify deficiencies, and we can fix deficiencies quickly through the test programmes. Each fix goes to Air Test and Evaluation Squadron 31 (VX-31) the developmental test unit based at Naval Air Station Patuxent River and Naval Air Weapons Station China Lake, and their sister operational test squadron VX-9 to quickly identify problems with a fix before the tested software is sent to the fleet.

"The main driver behind the incremental three-part test-and-release plan was to support the urgent fleet needs for the AIM-174 missile, LRASM 1.1, IRST, Small Diameter Bomb II, Advanced Anti-Radiation Guided Missile-Extended Range, and the Joint Advanced Tactical Missile for the F/A-18E/F Super Hornet, and the ALQ-249 NGJ-MB on the EA-18G Growler, and the development timelines."

In April 2023, the US Navy fielded SCS H18 Release 1 to support LRASM 1.1. This was followed by Release 2, and then Release 3 in September, 2024. PMA-265 will now release a software tape for software maintenance. Each H18 Release improved stability and added capabilities.

Explaining further, Howe said: "In parallel, we were doing the agile software development. The first agile CIDD build, dubbed CD25, is scheduled to be released in the fall, 2025 timeframe. When CD25 is released, we'll be able to quickly release each successive build to add stability and capability. CD25 will support the global lightning BLOS SATCOM capability which is expected to come out this fall."

GBU-53/B SDB II

In April 2024, the US Navy announced that a US Navy and US Air Force team, along with the test community and fleet stakeholders would complete two additional operational test events with the

Left: Landing signal officers direct an F/A-18E Super Hornet assigned to Strike Fighter Squadron 136 (VFA-136) 'Knighthawks' from the landing signal platform on the flight deck of the Nimitz-class aircraft carrier USS *Harry S. Truman* (CVN 75). The carrier was underway in the Atlantic Ocean during COMPTUEX, an intense, multi-week exercise designed to fully integrate a carrier strike group as a cohesive, multi-mission fighting force.
US Navy/Mass Communication Specialist Matthew Nass

Below: An F/A-18E Super Hornet assigned to Strike Fighter Squadron 211 (VFA-211) 'Fighting Checkmates' in a bolter from the flight deck of the Nimitz-class aircraft carrier USS *Theodore Roosevelt* (CVN 71) underway in the US 5th Fleet area of operations.
US Navy

F/A-18 SUPER HORNET

Left: **An F/A-18F Super Hornet assigned to Air Test and Evaluation Squadron 9 (VX-9) 'Vampires' flies away from a US Air Force KC-135 Stratotanker after aerial refuelling during Exercise Rim of the Pacific 2024 in and around the Hawaiian Islands. The world's largest international maritime exercise involved 29 nations, 40 surface ships, three submarines, land forces from 14 nations, more than 150 aircraft and 25,000 personnel.** US Air Force/SSgt Tiffany Emery

GBU-53/B Small Diameter Bomb Increment II and the Super Hornet before achieving initial operational capability in 2024.

The GBU-53/B SDB II is an air-launched, precision-strike, standoff weapon designed to defeat moving and fixed targets in adverse weather conditions. Using a GPS/INS system to guide to the vicinity of a moving target, the weapon has the capability to receive updated target coordinates mid-flight via two-way datalink (Link-16 or UHF) communications. Using these network options, SDB II allows airborne or ground controllers the ability to send in-flight target updates and the capability to abort a mission post-release.

According to the FY2023 annual report released by the Director, Operational Test & Evaluation, the Small Diameter Bomb Increment II programme continued integration testing on the F/A-18 Super Hornet, F-35B, and F-35C Lightning II aircraft. Cryptographic information delivery, mission planning, and operational flight program [OFP] software compatibility continued to delay test progress. This resulted in only one F-35 test mission and three Super Hornet missions in FY2023. The programme now anticipates SDB II initial operational capability on the Super Hornet in FY2024 and on the F-35B and F-35C in FY2025.

Left: **A US Air Force KC-135 Stratotanker aerial refuels a US Navy F/A-18F Super Hornet over the Pacific Ocean near Hawaii during Exercise Rim of the Pacific 2024.** US Air Force/SSgt Tiffany Emery

F/A-18 SUPER HORNET

Above: **An F/A-18E Super Hornet assigned to Strike Fighter Squadron 192 (VFA-192) 'Golden Dragons' loaded with an inert AIM-174B missile prior to launch from the USS Nimitz-class aircraft carrier USS Abraham Lincoln (CVN-70).** Screen grab/60 Minutes Australia

In FY2020, the US Navy initiated a quick reaction assessment (QRA) to integrate SDB II into the F/A-18 Super Hornet. DOT&E approved a six-event QRA test plan, which the navy expects to complete in FY2024. During FY2023, the navy conducted two live-fly operational tests for SDB II integration on the Super Hornet.

Concurrent software developments delayed test missions and limited new testing using the OFPs and mission planning environment (MPE) software intended for operational fielding. Operational test agencies will test these capabilities during the three remaining Super Hornet operational test missions.

Despite ongoing efforts to modernise encryption keys and update aircraft, weapon, and mission planning software, the programme has not yet demonstrated operational effectiveness on the Super Hornet. The Super Hornet and the F-35 have been unable to use the weapon's full new functionality with the aircraft OFPs and MPE software intended for operational fielding.

The FY2022 annual report highlighted a hardware issue affecting Super Hornet SDB II employment during bomb rack ejection. The Super Hornet programme implemented a materiel solution last year; however, further data analysis is required to determine whether this sufficiently reduces the likelihood of degrading weapon performance.

Cryptographic key loading and mission planning for the SDB II delayed integration testing on the F/A-18 Super Hornet and the F-35. Synchronising cryptographic keys across the weapon, the MPE, and the key filler devices is a complex process that involves several management nodes outside the Super Hornet programme office.

Ongoing Super Hornet Testing at VX-23

Discussing test activity with the F/A-18 Super Hornet at Air Test and Evaluation Squadron 23 (VX-23), test weapon systems officer Lieutenant Pat Lyons said: "We are testing the AAQ-28 LITENING targeting pod including shape testing for carrier suitability. VX-23 has just completed IRST carrier suitability testing to evaluate how the IRST system responds to the different forces encountered during a catapult shot and a trap. Typically, most carrier suitability testing is undertaken using the TC-7 steam catapult and the Mk7 arresting gear installed on the field here at Pax River. Typically, most carrier suitability testing is signed off at the field. We put the Super Hornet and IRST to the limits without having to be underway on an aircraft carrier and the hazards that come with that, for example, increasing the aircraft's weight for the cat shot and trap. We also deployed the IRST to a carrier during Exercise Valiant Shield to gain an operational perspective of how it's performing, and it's performing astronomically well. We've also completed software regression testing of the IRST's integration on the Super Hornet."

The IRST is a passive, long-range sensor system that uses infrared search and track technology to detect and track airborne threats with weapon-quality accuracy, which increases pilot reaction time and improves aircraft survivability. On the F/A-18 Super Hornet, IRST is mounted in the nose section of a centreline fuel tank.

Discussing other ongoing testing, Lieutenant Lyons said: "VX-23 regularly undertakes system interoperability testing with other types of aircraft assigned to Pax River, not least the F-35. We're able to set up events to evaluate different systems that different platforms bring to the game, and how they interact with each other."

Discussing ongoing test activities for the Block 3 Super Hornet, Davide Howe said: "Data networking, BLOS, and ADVEW will be integrated in addition to the Block 3 capability. We're trying to ensure that software and the basic functionalities of each system are relevant on both the Block 2 and the Block 3 aircraft."

AIM-174B

TV footage which aired on *60 minutes Australia* in July 2024 covered Exercise Rim of the Pacific 2024 (RIMPAC) and showed an AIM-174 missile loaded on an F/A-18E Super Hornet assigned to Strike Fighter Squadron 192 (VFA-192) as part of Carrier Air Wing 2 (CVW-2). Davide Howe confirmed that testing of the AIM-174 missile was complete, and that the missile type is in operation. Basic weapons separation, flight loads, dynamics, vibration,

F/A-18 SUPER HORNET

Left: **EA-18G Growlers assigned to Air Test and Evaluation Squadron 9 (VX-9) 'Vampires' fly off the wing of a US Air Force KC-135 Stratotanker over the Pacific Ocean near Hawaii during Exercise Rim of the Pacific 2024. Both aircraft are loaded with ALQ-249 Next-Generation Jammer Mid-Band pods.** US Air Force/SSgt Tiffany Emery

fatigue testing was completed by VX-23 at Pax River.

VX-23's mission is to support the RDT&E of fixed wing tactical aircraft by providing aircraft and pilot assets, maintenance services, safety oversight and facility support for these efforts. Primary areas of support include flying qualities and performance evaluations, shipboard suitability, ordnance compatibility and ballistic efforts, reliability, and maintainability assessments.

The aircraft component of weapons testing for a missile like the AIM-174 includes pre-flight ground vibration and structural loads, flight envelope loads, performance, aeroelasticity and handling qualities.

The missile component of the testing includes the armament control system, flutter, aircraft and store loads, stability, and control, flying qualities, performance, vibration, aeroacoustics, thermal and safe separation.

Responding to media enquiries about the AIM-174 sighting, a US Navy spokesperson said: "The SM-6 Air Launched Configuration [ALC] was developed as part of the SM-6 family of missiles and is operationally deployed in the navy today."

Two versions of the AIM-174 were noted during RIMPAC, a permanent special test missile, labelled the NAIM-174B, and a dummy air test missile, labelled the DATM-174B.

To our knowledge, no air intercept missile, labelled AIM-174B, was seen during RIMPAC, possibly indicating that the missiles seen were deployed for the exercise in support of a NAVAIR test programme.

RTX says the SM-6 missile is three missiles in one. It's the only weapon that can perform anti-air warfare, anti-surface warfare, and ballistic missile defence or sea-based terminal missions.

Referred to as the SM-6 air launched configuration and designated the AIM-174B in the air-to-air configuration, the missile reportedly uses an X-band receiver for guidance provided by the radar system of either of the US Navy's current strike fighters: the F/A-18 Super Hornet's APG-79 or the F-35C Lightning II's APG-81 AESA radar. Fire control data can also be provided via the Naval Integrated Fire Control–Counter Air (NIFC-CA) datalink, a system fitted to Super Hornet fighters and E-2D Hawkeye control aircraft.

Photographs seen to date show a single AIM-174 missile loaded on inner underwing pylons, of which there are four on a Super Hornet. The SM-6 missile's range is quoted by some publications as 130nm and 240nm by others. Specialist media outlets specify the SM-6 with a derivative of the seeker used by the RTX AIM-120 AMRAAM missile, no doubt an enlarged device given the difference in missile fuselage diameter between an AIM-120 and an AIM-174.

The US Navy's key requirement for employing the AIM-174 missile is to enable prosecution of targets positioned at greater ranges from the aircraft carrier than those available with the venerable AIM-120 AMRAAM.

Below: **An aircraft director guides the pilot of an F/A-18E Super Hornet, assigned to Strike Fighter Squadron 151 (VFA-151) 'Vigilantes' on the flight deck of the Nimitz-class aircraft carrier USS *Abraham Lincoln* (CVN 72) underway in the US 3rd Fleet area of operations.** US Navy/Mass Communication Specialist Seaman Nathaly Cruz

MQ-25 STINGRAY

STINGRAY

Naval Air Systems Command and Boeing's Phantom Works are currently developing a new weapon system that's set to change many of the established cultures of military aviation: the carrier-based MQ-25 Stingray autonomous aerial refuelling unmanned air vehicle.

US NAVY CAPTAIN Dan Fucito is the US Navy's programme manager for unmanned carrier aviation programmes with PMA-268. The largest programme under his watch is the MQ-25 Stingray air vehicle and the MD-5 ground station, together with all the modifications required onboard the US Navy's carriers and shore-based facilities for control of the MQ-25. He took command of PMA-268 in February 2023.

Following the US Navy's decision to lead the system integration effort for the MQ-25, PMA-268 is working with Boeing Defense based in St Louis and Lockheed Martin which is building the MD-5 ground control station. Lockheed Martin provides the desks, controls, consoles, and server racks, which the navy integrates into its command-and-control structure to create the MD-5 ground control system.

"Every hole in the aircraft is pre-drilled. All the parts come pre-cut, and it's supposed to be an assembly procedure, as opposed to a fabrication procedure. We worked through quality issues with the suppliers and most of the quality issues are now resolved. Consequently, MQ-25 air vehicles are now moving along the production line and most of the challenges we are now encountering are in production because this aircraft has never been built before.

"Five aircraft are currently in production, EDM1, EDM2, EDM3, EDM4 and SDTA1. SDTA1 is fully instrumented with over 800 strain gauges to measure all the forces on the aircraft. We've completed the test setup and started static testing with SDTA1 in the last week of August. The start of bending and flexing the aircraft is a significant moment for the programme. We have high confidence in the aircraft's design, but it's reassuring to acquire test data to prove that.

"As each aircraft rolls off the St Louis production line, it will be ground-transported to MidAmerica airport from where it will complete its first flight. Of the first three aircraft, the order will be EDM3, EDM1, and then EDM2 a little bit later. We will accept each aircraft at Boeing's St Louis facility in January 2025 followed by ground testing at MidAmerica aircraft, and then first flights which are planned for summer 2025.

"EDM3 is likely to roll-out first. EDM1 must undergo load calibration because it's a fully instrumented aircraft. It will stay at St Louis for longer while the strain gauges are calibrated. EDM3 will be delivered to flight test by early January 2025 and its first flight is scheduled for the summer of 2025. EDM1 will be ferried to Pax in mid-2025. Later in 2025 we'll ferry them to Lakehurst for catapult and the resting

Above: **T1 N234MQ (s/n 00001) on its first wheels-up flight from MidAmerica Airport. The shadow cast shows the air vehicle's chine, the longitudinal line of sharp change in the cross-section profile of the fuselage.** Boeing Phantom Works

gear testing. Initial sea trials are scheduled to begin in the late spring of 2026. We intend to deliver the last EDM aircraft by the end of 2027.

"We're planning to fly EDM1, EDM3, and eventually EDM2 and EDM4 at Patuxent River where we will conduct air mechanical testing, envelope expansion, shore-based carrier suitability testing, and testing of the Joint Precision Approach and Landing System [JPALS]. The MQ-25 aircraft is the first ever to use the auto-land feature of the JPALS, which to date has shown great success in the lab. The MQ-25 will also undergo climatic chamber testing in the McKinley Climatic Laboratory at Eglin Air Force Base, Florida."

According to the Air Force Test Center: "Capabilities available at the McKinley climatic laboratory help engineers ensure maximum reliability and operational capability of complex systems. The laboratory has five testing chambers:

Below: **This shot of T1 in level flight shows the flaperons on the most outward part of the wing.**
Boeing Phantom Works

the main chamber; the equipment test chamber; the sun, wind, rain, and dust chamber; the salt fog chamber; and the altitude chamber. The main chamber, measuring 252ft wide, 260ft deep and 70ft high, is the largest environmental chamber in the world. It can create temperatures between -65 to 165°F and can simulate climatic conditions including heat, snow, rain, wind, sand, and dust. The sun, wind, rain, and dust chamber produce ambient or hot test conditions, creates wind-blown rain at up to 25in per hour and heavy sand and dust storms. The salt fog chamber which measures approximately 55ft long, 16ft wide and 16ft high, has two steam-fed heat exchangers that create the temperature to perform the salt fog test."

Explaining more testing, Captain Fucito said: "MQ-25 catapult, arresting gear and jet blast testing will be undertaken at Naval Air Engineering Station Lakehurst, New Jersey, followed by sea trials, which are planned on board an aircraft carrier in 2026. So, eight to ten months of flight testing at Pax River and then aboard a carrier which will complete the launch recovery bulletin, which authorises the aircraft to be launched from, and recovered to the ship. Once, we get the launch and recovery bulletins integrated into the fleet we can deploy the MQ-25 for the first time.

"Work on the Unmanned Aviation Mission Control Station [UMCS], and the Unmanned Air Warfare Center [UAWC], which is the ground control station installed on the carriers is proceeding well. We're working with Lockheed Martin on the ground control station together with NAVAIR's command and control PMAs to fully integrate the MQ-25-specific systems with the command-and-control structure.

"Since none of these systems are currently in operation, almost everything we do is unprecedented. We made history earlier this month, when our first UAWC went live on-board the USS *George HW Bush* (CVN 77) at Naval Base Norfolk. All

MQ-25 STINGRAY

Left: **T1 undergoing initial ground testing on an imitation catapult at Boeing's St Louis, Missouri facility. Note the Phantom Works logo on the side of the forward fuselage.** Boeing Phantom Works

Right: **Touch down at MidAmerica St Louis Airport, Illinois at the end of T1's maiden flight on September 19, 2019.** Boeing Phantom Works

Below: **T1 flew its September 19, 2019, maiden flight with the landing gear extended, common practice for initial test flights.** Boeing Phantom Works

the server racks are installed and the UAWC is connected to the carrier's C4I system with all the stations powered up. We're working through the initial tests which will form the baseline from which we will advance our testing later this year when we plan to radiate and control from the carrier, as opposed to a shore-based control station.

"The UAWC is a permanent feature of the ship. Luckily, we didn't have to cut the ship to get our equipment in, but we did have to cut the ship to install some of the support equipment. We're talking 1,000lb server racks rolling down the pathways on the ship, so once they are in, they are permanently installed.

"We also have shore-based hardware. In April, we successfully demonstrated end-to-end flight operations using the first build of software in our systems test and integration lab [STIL], a high-fidelity hardware-in-the-loop lab here at Pax. Using the STIL, we were able to simulate air vehicle start-up and withdraw the commands. We transferred that to a real deck handling device and simulated aircraft movement around the airfield and transfer to the control station, simulated a take-off, simulated control of emission, and then simulated return to base, landing, and shutdown. We were able to exercise the systems using hardware and software, often over the air links between antennas here at Pax.

"The MQ-25 will be the first Group 5 UAV, one that's about the size of an E-2 Hawkeye aircraft, to be fully integrated on an aircraft carrier. The intent is to operate the MQ-25 alongside manned aircraft without any of the special handling that most of the unmanned aircraft require today. So that's the challenge facing the team.

"In the future, other programmes will be able to build off the MQ-25, whether that's a collaborative combat aircraft or some type of unmanned aircraft which the navy will decide to integrate into the air wing of the future."

CBARS Competition

Based on the US government's acquisition strategy approved in April 2017, the MQ-25 programme is an evolution from the previous Unmanned Carrier Launched Airborne Surveillance and Strike (UCLASS) programme, and the Next Generation Air Dominance (NGAD) family of systems.

MQ-25 STINGRAY

Above: **T1 positioned with the forward launch and aft holdback bars lowered over the imitation catapult's shuttle track.** Boeing Phantom Works

Documents from each programme highlighted the need for carrier-based aerial refuelling and persistent ISR capabilities to support the Carrier Strike Group (CSG), requirements that were set out in guidance issued by the Joint Requirements Oversight Council (JROC). On July 21, 2017, the JROC validated the capability development document for the MQ-25 Carrier Based Aerial Refueling System, or CBARS.

Designed to be sustainable on board an aircraft carrier and from shore bases, the MQ-25 system is comprised of three major architectural segments. All three segments are managed by PMA-268, the lead systems integrator (LSI).

- The air segment includes the MQ-25 air vehicle and associated support and handling equipment including the deck handling system, spares, and repair materials.
- The control system and connectivity (CS&C) segment includes the Unmanned carrier aviation Mission Control System (UMCS); its associated communication equipment; the mission support functionality of the Distributed Common Ground Station-Navy (DCGS-N), the US Navy's primary intelligence, surveillance, reconnaissance and targeting system; the network-based interface and routing equipment required to control the Stingray; and all required modifications to existing networks and C4I system infrastructure.
- The CVN (aircraft carrier) segment comprises the ships' spaces allocated to unmanned carrier aviation, installed ship systems, and modifications necessary for interface with the air and CS&C segments. CVN systems important to the MQ-25 include those

Above: **An artist's impression of the Lockheed Martin proposal for the CBARS programme, shown on a catapult ready for launch.** Lockheed Martin

Right: **When T1 entered the initial flight test programme, the Phantom Works logo was removed from the forward fuselage on each side.** Boeing Phantom Works

Left: **Combined system and taxi testing at Boeing's St Louis facility. This shot shows the fuselage cross section form, the bulges of the wing joints housing the actuators and hydraulically-actuated pins that lock the wings in place, and the pitch of the tail surfaces of the V-tail.** Boeing Phantom Works

supporting aircraft launch and recovery, data dissemination systems (including radio terminals and antennas), and deck operations systems. Ship installation requires considerable work to re-model nearly 85m² of space on board the carrier to house the UMCS.

Systems specific to carrier flight deck operations include a tail hook for arrested landings; foldable wings to minimise the air vehicle's parking footprint on the flight deck; design features that ease maintenance; and on-deck control systems that integrate with systems currently used on Nimitz and Ford-class carriers.

Concepts for the long defunct UCLASS programme were deemed too difficult and challenging given the number of new technologies involved, all of which required evaluation. Consequently, NAVAIR's PMA-268 implemented a restart to evaluate the art of the possible for introducing something so new as the MQ-25, and to explore concepts of operation.

In 2016, US Congress had appropriated PMA-268 a congressional plus-up award for four contractors each capable of developing a UAS suitable for the CBARS requirements: Boeing, General Atomics, Lockheed Martin, and Northrop Grumman.

Each contractor presented PMA-268 with ideas about how they were to mature their own technologies and concepts prior to receiving their share of the congressional plus-up award: a means of funding their respective concept development programmes through mid-2018. At that point with details, including the giveaway fuel load and ranges of each of the concepts submitted, PMA-268 conducted a tanker trade study which help conclude its requirements for the CBARS programme.

PMA-268 released the draft air system engineering, manufacturing, and development (EMD) request for proposal (RFP) in July 2017 and released the final EMD RFP in early October 2017. Shortly

MQ-25 STINGRAY

afterwards, Northrop Grumman dropped out of the competition, citing an inability to meet the navy's specification and deliver a profit.

Less than eight months after receiving qualified proposals, PMA-268 awarded the EMD contract to Boeing in August, 2018.

T1 and Flight Testing

Phantom Works, Boeing's advanced prototyping division, started building air vehicle T1 in 2012. The design features a blended wing-body-tail air foil with folding, high-aspect-ratio wings, and a V-tail. Its configuration reflects the long-endurance mission requirements of the UCLASS programme, particularly the long thin wings. Phantom Works finished the first iteration in 2014 as part of its design proposal for the UCLASS programme.

Air vehicle T1 has the same outer mould line and the same engine to production standard MQ-25s. Consequently, some aspects of testing already undertaken with T1 will not require repeating with a production standard air vehicle.

The objective of the MQ-25 test programme is to evaluate system maturity and technical performance of the aerial refuelling role, both mission and recovery tanking.

Initial ground testing with T1, including communications integration, towing,

Above: **An artist's impression of General Atomics' proposal for the CBARS programme, shown aerial refuelling an F/A-18 Super Hornet from the single ARS mounted under the left wing.**
General Atomics

Left: **This top-down shot of T1 attached to the imitation catapult's shuttle shows the embedded engine intake a top the fuselage, and the airfoil of the wing.**

MQ-25 STINGRAY

UNMANNED CARRIER AVIATION MISSION CONTROL SYSTEM

Designated the MD-5 A/B (ship/shore), the UMCS is the US Navy's core such system, comprising scalable computing and display hardware, open architecture-based mission systems software, communication equipment, and connectivity to networking environments as required for both CVN and shore-based control of the MQ-25A.

An MD-5 A/B control station comprises six OJ-845 common display systems, two UYQ-122 common processing systems, one network processing group, and one integrated communication system.

Lockheed Martin is developing the MD-5 and PMA-268 is developing the operating software. PMA-268 is also responsible for all modifications required to shore-based and carrier infrastructure. The latter includes integration of NAVAIR-developed software with Boeing's air vehicle OFP, the network, and the command, control and communication systems that will enable the MQ-25 to operate within the carrier environment.

The UMCS hardware builds on Naval Sea Systems Command's common display system and common processing system from DDG-1000 Zumwalt-class destroyer and other Aegis-equipped ships.

combined system, and taxi, began almost immediately following contract award at Boeing's facilities in St Louis, Missouri.

In April 2019, Boeing trucked T1 to MidAmerica St Louis Airport in Illinois (the commercial side of Scott Air Force Base) to conduct the first phases of flight testing. T1's maiden flight took place there on September 19, 2019. The company chose MidAmerica because of hangar, runway, taxiway, and air space availability.

Phase one of initial T1 testing concluded in the spring of 2020 during which the team had worked through test points designed to evaluate guidance and control, basic flying qualities, aerodynamic performance of the air vehicle, altitudes and air speeds, and performance of the engine, all in a clean configuration.

Evaluation of flight and aerodynamic performance is based on flight test data captured by the instrumentation installed on T1.

After completing 12 flights and amassing approximately 30 flight hours, in the spring of 2020 T1 entered a period of modification to integrate a Cobham 31-301-7 buddy aerial refuelling store (ARS) under the left wing. The modification was required because T1 was originally developed to meet the requirements of UCLASS which did not include under wing pylons used to carry stores.

Modifications included hardware installation, software updates to enable operation of the ARS, and upgrade of the ground control station (GCS) to support the aerial refuelling mission.

Post-modification, T1 entered phase two of its test programme. This started with a rigorous modelling, analysis and ground-based test programme including software integration, functionality checks and multiple taxi tests to ensure quality and integrity before flight.

On December 9, T1 made its first flight with an aerial refuelling store on its right under-wing pylon. During the 2.5-hour first flight, the test team's objective was to gather data about aerodynamics effects of the ARS at various points in the flight envelope. The flight was conducted by Boeing's test pilots controlling T1 from a ground control station located at MidAmerica airport. Navy test team members participated in all Boeing-led T1 test events including air vehicle pilot operators (AVPOs) who were authorised to sit in the second and third GCS seats as observers to gain valuable early experience. Seat two was occupied by a pilot who monitored the flight and assisted Boeing's AVO pilot-in-command, while the test-unique seat three was occupied by a test observer. Because T1 is a Boeing-owned aircraft, the AVPO pilot-in-command was a Boeing test pilot.

Separately, navy AVPOs assigned to the developmental and operational squadrons (VX-23 and VX-1) were already participating in MQ-25 simulator-based training. This effort was designed to teach the AVPOs how to operate the aircraft from the GCS through start-up procedures to shut-down.

Right: **Another top-down shot shows the fuselage plan form, the engine intake's curved articulation, and the flaperons' position on the wings.**

MQ-25 STINGRAY

The initial focus of the testing was on the guidance and control of the air vehicle with the ARS installed, checking functionality of extending and retracting the hose from the ARS, and determining the behaviour of the hose and basket in T1's wake. The test team had to assess the necessary flight clearances and procedures required to engage the ARS basket, known as plugs.

Initial air wake surveys with an F/A-18 Super Hornet flying behind the air vehicle in a receiver position and potential plug testing were conducted at Boeing's facility at MidAmerica Airport in the same FAA-approved airspace used for T1 testing.

By January 12, 2021, T1 had flown 14 flights and amassed nearly 35 hours, a long way from the end game.

T1 continued flying to include engine and Joint Precision Approach and Landing System (JPALS) functionality testing. To enable propulsion testing, T1's AE3007N engine was fitted with additional instrumentation to validate its performance and evaluate its characteristics as installed in T1.

JPALS functionality testing required T1 to undergo a second modification period for installation of the anti-jam encrypted datalink required to connect software and receiver hardware on the air vehicle to GPS sensors, antennas, and equipment on the aircraft carrier. JPALS is a software-based, high-integrity differential GPS navigation and precision approach landing system that guides aircraft onto Nimitz and Ford-class aircraft carriers in all weather and surface conditions up to the rough waters of sea state 5. It uses an encrypted, jam-proof data link to connect to software and receiver hardware on the aircraft and an array of GPS sensors, mast-mounted antennas, and shipboard receivers.

T1's involvement in the test programme culminated with its hoisting aboard an aircraft carrier to test the deck handling and control station systems.

Buddy ARS and Aerial Refuelling Procedures

According to Cobham, the ARS is mounted on an ejector rack by two lugs spaced 30in apart. The store has an internal capacity of 250 US gal and is capable of pumping fuel to a receiver aircraft at the rate of 180/minute with a drogue pressure of 0.2 to 0.4 N/mm². A ram air turbine drives a variable displacement hydraulic pump when the store is activated. Hydraulic power generated by the pump provides the power to drive the hose reel and fuel pump motors. The ARS provides hose guillotine, jettison, and sealing; pod jettison; and fuel dump emergency provisions.

Cobham's 31-301-7 buddy Aerial Refuelling Store is already in service with US Navy F/A-18 Super Hornet strike fighter squadrons. PMA-268 developed a concept of operations for aerial refuelling from the MQ-25 involved single drogue refuelling from the air vehicle and the ARS, and followed the same procedures as currently used by Super Hornets.

According to the F/A-18 Super Hornet NATOPS (Naval Air Training and Operating Procedures Standardization) flight manual "a sharp lookout doctrine must be maintained during aerial refuelling due to the precise flying imposed on both the tanker aircrew and receiver pilots. Other aircraft in a formation may assist the tanker aircrew in maintaining a sharp lookout. Refuelling altitudes and airspeeds are dictated by receiver and/or tanker characteristics balanced with operational needs. This typically covers a practical envelope from the surface to 35,000ft and 180 to 300kts (while engaged), depending on the specific variant of ARS in use. Using ARS characteristics for the Super Hornet provided an indication of the operating limitations of the combined MQ-25-ARS system.

Above and right: **Boeing and Naval Air Systems Command flew T1 test with an aerial refuelling store loaded on the left side under-wing pylon for the first time on December 9, 2020.** Boeing/Dave Preston

"Aerial refuelling can be accomplished at altitudes between 500 and 35,000ft. In operation the ARS power can be switched on with the RAM air turbine un-feathered between 180 to 300kts, the hose can be extended at airspeeds between 180 to 275kts, fuel can be transferred between 180 and 300kts (depending on the ARS variant), and the hose can be retracted between 180 to 275kts depending on the altitude and ARS variant.

"When the pilot of the receiver aircraft is cleared to commence an approach and the aerial refuelling checklist is complete, the receiver pilot should assume a ready position 10 to 15ft in trail of the drogue, with the aerial refuelling probe in line both horizontally and vertically.

"Once the receiver aircraft is in a stabilized position, the receiver pilot must trim the aircraft and make sure the ARS

Left and right: **Ongoing flight testing of T1 will evaluate the aerodynamics of the air vehicle and the aerial refuelling store at various points of the flight envelope, eventually progressing to extension and retraction of the hose and drogue used for refuelling.**
Boeing/Kevin Flynn

MQ-25 STINGRAY

Above: **T1 is given operating directions on the flight deck aboard the aircraft carrier USS *George H.W. Bush* (CVN 77).**
US Navy/Mass Communication Specialist 3rd Class Brandon Roberson

ready light (amber) is on. Referencing the probe and drogue for alignment, the receiver pilot must increase power to establish a 3 to 5 knot closure rate. The receiver pilot must avoid an excessive closure rate, this may cause a violent hose whip following contact and/or increase the danger of structural damage to the aircraft in the event of misalignment. Similarly, an insufficient closure rate results in the receiver pilot fencing with the drogue as it oscillates near the aircraft nose.

"The receiver pilot must make small corrections during the approach phase using the rudder pedals for lateral misalignment and longitudinal stick for vertical misalignment. "Lateral stick inputs should be avoided as they cause both vertical and lateral probe displacement. During the final phase of the approach, the drogue tends to move up and to the right as it passes the nose of the receiver aircraft due to the aircraft-to-drogue air stream interaction.

"A missed approach should be executed if the receiver probe and the drogue basket cannot be properly aligned during the final phase of the approach; the receiver probe passes forward of the drogue basket; the receiver probe impinges on the rim of the drogue basket; or an unsafe condition develops. To execute a missed approach, the receiver aircraft pilot should reduce power and back off from the tanker with a 3 to 5 knot opening rate.

"When the receiver probe engages the basket (a contact), it seats itself into the

Right: **A sailor repositions T1 on the flight deck aboard the aircraft carrier USS *George H.W. Bush* (CVN 77).**
US Navy/Mass Communication Specialist 3rd Class Brandon Roberson

MQ-25 STINGRAY

Left: **The production-standard MQ-25's initial operating capability (IOC) as an aerial refuelling tanker will extend the range, operational capability and power projection of the Carrier Air Wing and Carrier Strike Group.** US Navy/Mass Communication Specialist 3rd Class Brandon Roberson

reception coupling and a slight ripple is evident in the refuelling hose. The drogue and hose must be pushed forward 5ft by the receiver aircraft before fuel transfer can be started.

"This position is evident by the tanker ready light (amber) going out, and the (green) fuel transfer light coming on. During refuelling, the receiver aircraft pilot must maintain a position directly behind and slightly below the tanker aircraft. The receiver aircraft disengages by reducing power to open from the tanker at 3 to 5 knots. Disengagement must be made straight back, parallel to the tanker flight path, maintaining a constant separation rate until clear, and descending along the natural trail angle of the hose to prevent damage to the tanker and/or receiver aircraft. The receiver aircraft's aerial refuelling probe separates from the reception coupling when the hose reaches full extension.

"One advisory. When installed on an F/A-18 Super Hornet tanker, the ARS hose/drogue/coupling exhibits a strong tendency to re-centre in its natural trail position. Off-centre disconnects may result in drogue contact and damage to the receiver aircraft and should be avoided.

"Given the MQ-25 is an unmanned platform, when the procedures outlined above are undertaken the AVPOs will rely on a set of aft-facing cameras for visual reference, and voice communications with the receiver aircraft pilot. Not only is this process remarkable involving manned fighter aircraft flying in very close proximity to an unmanned air vehicle flown by aircrew located in a UMCS on board an aircraft carrier, but it is also equally remarkable because of the technology and systems involved and made for an interesting flight test programme."

Future Test Phases

PMA-268 believes that having T1 available for testing years before the first EDM comes off Boeing's St Louis production line enabled the test team to discover issues early so they could be corrected during the development of the EDM air vehicles, thereby reducing risk. For example, an icing susceptibility issue with the air data probe system was identified. Boeing designed a different air data probe which was fitted during production of the EDM air vehicles.

EDM1 and EDM2 will be dedicated to flight sciences testing fitted with similar instrumentation to T1. EDM1 will undergo all aspects of a standard flight test programme followed by catapult launches and arrested landings.

EDM3 and EDM4 will be dedicated to mission systems, the air vehicle's effectiveness to the aerial refuelling role, and carrier suitability testing.

Any aircraft's all-up weight is an incredibly important design parameter for carrier suitability. The MQ-25 must be capable of fulfilling its tanking role despite the constraints imposed by maximum catapult shot weights and arrested recoveries from Nimitz- and Ford-class carriers. All-up weight was also constrained by the requirement for a fuel

Below: **Sailors and Boeing employees look for discrepancies in the positioning of T1 on the flight deck aboard the aircraft carrier USS *George H.W. Bush* (CVN 77).** US Navy/Mass Communication Specialist 3rd Class Brandon Roberson

MQ-25 STINGRAY

Left: **T1 on the flight deck aboard the aircraft carrier USS** *George H.W. Bush* **(CVN 77). The production-standard MQ-25 will be the world's first operational, carrier-based unmanned aircraft and is integral to the air wing of the future family of systems.**
US Navy/Mass Communication Specialist 3rd Class Hillary Becke

giveaway of 15,000lb at 500 miles from the carrier. By comparison, a Super Hornet holds a giveaway fuel load of 12,000lb on a two-hour cycle, 15,000lb on a normal cycle and 25,000lb on a short cycle.

The MQ-25 will also be tasked with recovery tanking, which involves having a tanker airborne in orbit close to the carrier while aircraft recover. This is a critical capability at night or when the weather conditions are bad with a pitching deck in heavy seas, such that pilots need to top up the tanks to afford further attempts to land on the flight deck.

During our interview, we asked Captain Fucito a series of questions which are set-out with his responses below.

Q: What was involved in the MQ-25 demonstration onboard USS *George H.W Bush* in 2021?

A: "In December 2021, the US Navy completed a demonstration using Boeing's MQ-25 prototype T1 on the USS *George H W Bush*. It laid the groundwork for deck operations and involved start-up, taxi, moving the air vehicle onto the catapult, checking of the jet blast deflector, moving the air vehicle out of the landing area, and around the carrier flight deck. We also completed day and night handling on board the USS *George H.W Bush*."

Q: What was involved in the evaluation of the deck handling system?

A: "During the demo, deck operators used Boeing's deck control device during all phases of the deck handling system evaluation. Operators working for Boeing stood next to navy taxi directors, the yellow shirts who move

Below: US Navy/Mass Communication Specialist 3rd Class Hillary Becke

US NAVY AND MARINE CORPS YEARBOOK **2024**

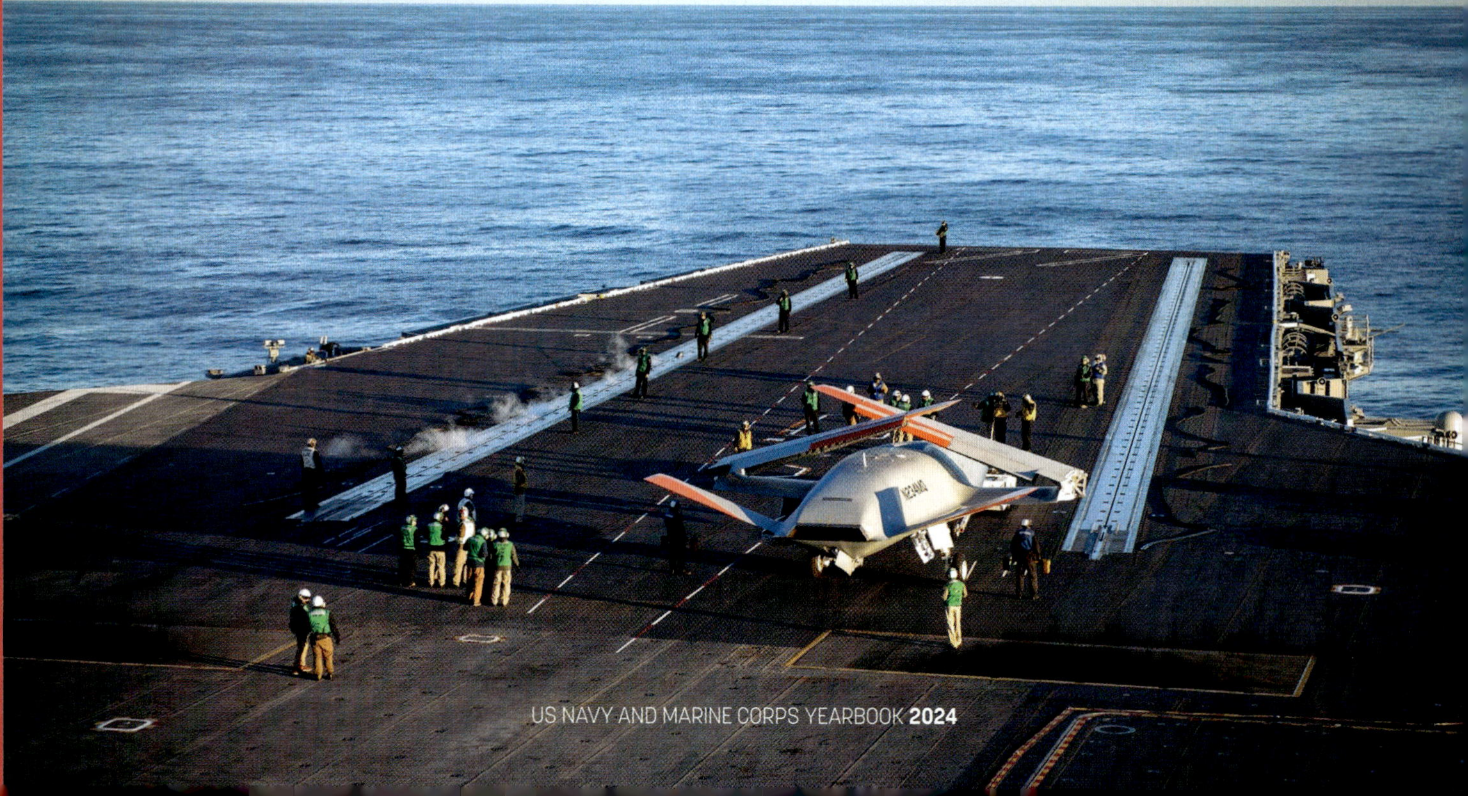

aircraft around the flight deck. For example, a taxi director gave the aircraft a spot number so that the deck handler could then use a deck control device to manoeuvre the aircraft around the carrier's flight deck."

Q: How does the Lockheed Martin MD-5 unmanned carrier aviation mission control system differ to Boeing's generic control system used to support T1?

A: "Boeing's control station was specific to aircraft T1, both components were prototypes. The MD-5 ground control system is developed by Lockheed Martin and the deck control device remains a Boeing product. The MD-5 is more mature and has more potential. Originally, the navy was planning to develop a common control system for unmanned carrier aviation but realised that Lockheed Martin had a system that would fit very well. In 2020, the navy shifted to using the MD-5 system, which is designed to plug into all the other command and control systems the navy intended to use."

Q: When did the MD-5 ground control station integrate with a simulated air vehicle in the System Test Integration Lab (STIL) at Pax River?

A: "The STIL lab has a production representative MD-5 ground control station, a vehicle management system computer, and a mission management system computer, with all the boxes laid out. These systems have been integrated since 2021. We have integrated fleet representative hardware with fleet representative software and used all the command-and-control links. We use hardware and software to provide a realistic surrogate for the air vehicle. Sometimes we use over-the-air transmission to make sure the antennas have the gain that we need, and we can get the beyond line-of-sight links we need using satellite communications. Testers use the fleet representative equipment in the STIL to evaluate the system and to see how they like it. Testers also make constructive changes to the integrated equipment to produce a more mature product up front, instead of waiting until the final aircraft configuration is rolled-out to test simulated flight using the air vehicle and associated switching connections for links to the aircraft."

Q: How many MQ-25 air vehicles will be involved in the flight test programme?

A: "T1 had a limited flight service life and doesn't have many hours left. I'm not sure T1 will ever fly again. Eventually we will have ten test aircraft: the static test aircraft, which we will also do drop testing with, four EDM models [EDM1-EDM4] and five system demonstration test aircraft [SDTA1-SDTA5], and we'll have a fatigue test article to check the overall fatigue life of the airframe.

Above: US Navy/Mass Communication Specialist 3rd Class Hillary Becke

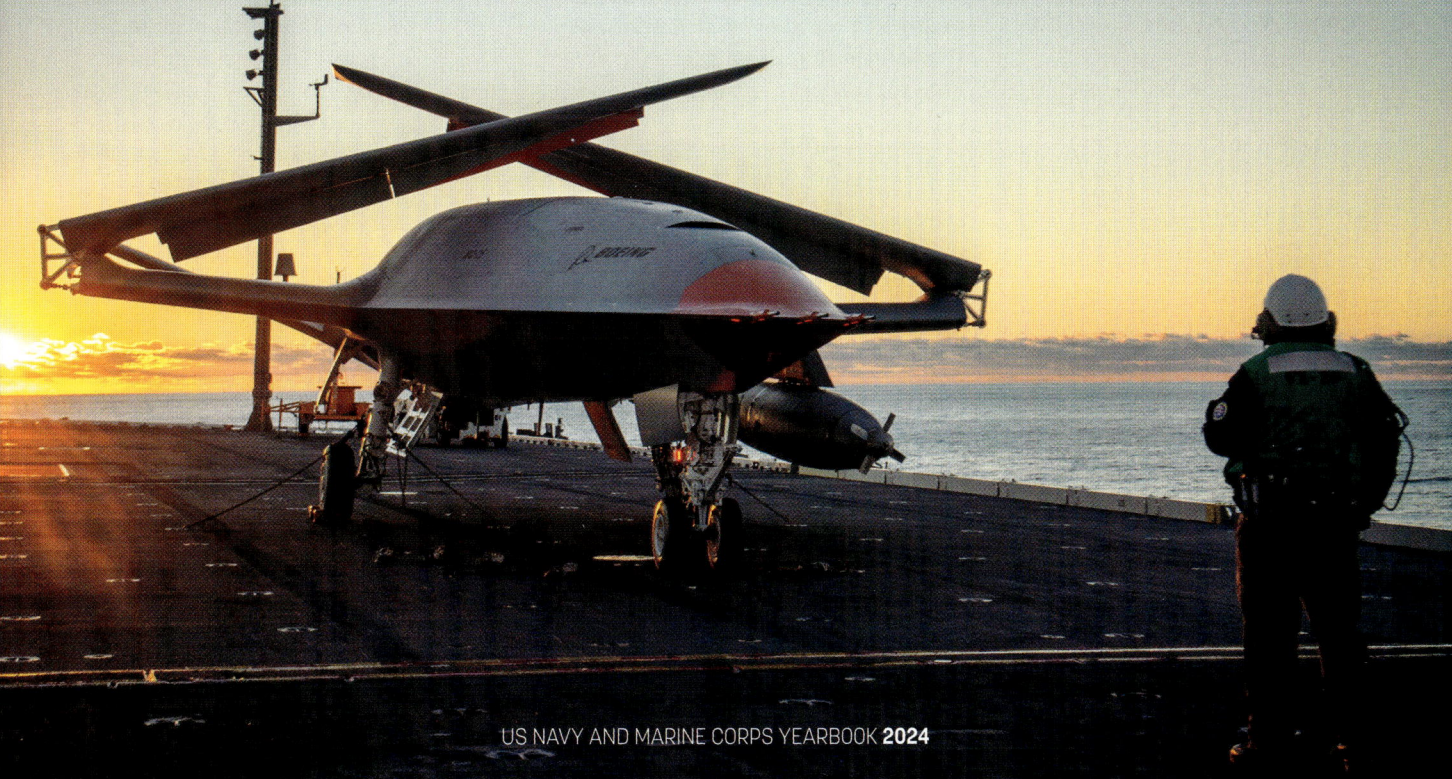

Below: PMA-268 completed a demonstration using Boeing's MQ-25 prototype T1 on the USS *George H. W. Bush* in December 2021. US Navy/Mass Communication Specialist 3rd Class Brandon Roberson

MQ-25 STINGRAY

MQ-25 air vehicle testing will be conducted by Air Test and Evaluation Squadron 23 (VX-23) and with representatives from Unmanned Air Test and Evaluation Squadron 24 (UX-24) will conduct testing of the ground control element."

Q: What major test events have been accomplished to date?

A: "We began formal system testing using Block 4 software in December 2023. We completed joint end-to-end system verification testing of the software for the ground control station and air vehicle, which involved Boeing, Lockheed Martin, and PMA-268. We have also completed an integration event of the Block 5 software, which included everything necessary for an MQ-25 air vehicle to go to the ship, and we're progressing toward our second joint system verification test later this year. To date, we've demonstrated successful integration for every phase of flight, including over 40 simulated carrier approaches with the JPALS system. We can meet all the requirements, for landing aboard a carrier including trapping in up to sea state five, which is heavy seas."

Q: What are the significant differences between T1 and an EDM model?

A: "Internal structures, fuel system design, communication and network architecture. T1 was a concept demonstrator. It carried the minimum amount of fuel required to do the aerodynamic shaping of the aircraft. The structure of an EDM MQ-25 is more robust inside to withstand catapult launches and carrier assessments. EDM aircraft have all the fuel systems, all the electrical systems, and the ability to move fuel around. And the biggest difference is the structure which is built to have the required service life. T1 was used to aerial refuel three major type model series aircraft, the F/A-18 Super Hornet, the F-35 Lightning II and the E-2D Hawkeye. The data collected from those events about the proof of concept of aerial refuelling, basket dynamics, and exhaust plume dynamics will be used in the flight test programme."

Q: The MQ-25 is intended to integrate manned and unmanned teaming [MUM-T] operations and to mature command, control, communications, and intelligence [C4I] technologies used by unmanned air vehicles, what is the current programme status of these capabilities?

Above: **PMA-268 started static testing with MQ-25 static test aircraft SDTA1 in the last week of August.** Naval Air Systems Command

Left: **The Unmanned Air Warfare Center dubbed the UAWC.** Naval Air Systems Command

A: "We are first and foremost integrating the digital backbone between the UAWC and the C4I. We have attempted to minimise bringing any new C4I solutions for the fleet and we're trying to plug into what the fleet already has. We are pioneering the modification of the carriers and optimising that design. Boeing has been doing some early MUM-T work between F/A-18 and MQ-25, establishing what can be done to possibly extend command and control, not just from the UAWC, but from manned aircraft, to improve how the MQ-25 responds and integrates with them."

Q: What is the status of the Navy's MUM-T operational concept?

A: "We're looking for the ability to directly re-task the MQ-25. Currently the UAV air vehicle pilots develop a flight plan. They can change the flight plan. But part of the MUM-T may come from the UAV or maybe from another entity if the MQ-25 must be re-tasked somewhere else. We're working on that concept using the existing communication networks. Our work is the first end-to-end test of integrated unmanned concepts afloat. Operational concepts are still very much under development."

Q: In April 2023, a UH-1Y helicopter completed an initial flight test to test the data transmission of the new mobile user objective system [MUOS] capability at Pax River, what

MQ-25 STINGRAY

Left: **The demonstration completed onboard the USS *George H. W. Bush* laid the groundwork for deck operations and involved start-up, taxi, moving the air vehicle onto the catapult, checking of the jet blast deflector, moving the air vehicle out of the landing area, and around the carrier flight deck.**
US Navy/Mass Communication Specialist 3rd Class Brandon Roberson

were the objectives and what did the test prove?

A: "This was an example of using a surrogate aircraft for proof of concept. During the test, the lab transmitted some data up to the UH-1Y. We proved that there was line of connectivity between the MUOS SATCOM and the receivers and that we could transmit data, receive data, and correct errors as required."

Q: How resilient was the communication link while the aircraft manoeuvred?

A: "A helicopter is much more manoeuvrable than an MQ-25, but you never know if you're going to blank, if you're going to break chain. The test objective was to establish the link and maintain the link on an airborne platform."

Q: Is the USS *George HW Bush*, the first carrier configured for MQ-25 operations, and what are the main components of work required to configure a carrier for those operations?

A: "USS *George H.W Bush* is the first carrier configured for MQ-25 operations. Modifications centre around the UAWC having all the proper elements fully connected, fully powered and the required space fully built so the control consoles, the server racks and the security elements are there for the air vehicle pilots to control the MQ-25."

AIR VEHICLE CONTROL

Using mouse and keyboard controls, the operator commands the air vehicle where it needs to go and inputs what it's required to do, and the system determines how to get there in the most safe and efficient way.

The air vehicle operator, either a warrant officer or an aviator, will use the MD-5 control station housed within the UAWC on the carrier throughout all stages of the mission from the catapult launch to the arrestment.

Prior to launch and landing, a deck handling operator, a 'yellow shirt', will use a deck control device to taxi the Stingray around the flight deck. Once the air vehicle is on the catapult, at some point the deck handling operator will hand-off to the air vehicle operator. After landing, the deck handling operator will assume control to taxi the air vehicle to its parking spot.

Below: **MQ-25 static test aircraft SDTA1 during hoisting in May, 2024.**
Naval Air Systems Command

US NAVY AND MARINE CORPS YEARBOOK **2024**

THE DESTINATION FOR AVIATION ENTHUSIASTS

Visit us today and discover all our publications

Aviation News is renowned for providing the best coverage of every branch of aviation.

Air International has established an unrivalled reputation for authoritative reporting across the full spectrum of aviation subjects.

SIMPLY SCAN THE **QR CODE** OF YOUR FAVOURITE TITLE ABOVE TO FIND OUT MORE!

FREE P&P* when you order

shop.keypublishing.com

Call +44 (0)1780 480404 *(Mon to Fri 9am - 5.30pm GMT)*

SUBSCRIBE TODAY!

Airforces Monthly is devoted to modern military aircraft and their air arms.

Combat Aircraft Journal is renowned for being America's best-selling military aviation magazine.

from our online shop...
/collections/subscriptions

*Free 2nd class P&P on all UK & BFPO orders. Overseas charges apply.

MARINE ALL-WEATHER FIGHTER ATTACK SQUADRON 224

FIGHTING

Marine All Weather Fighter Attack Squadron 224 (VMFA[AW]-224) 'Fighting Bengals' is the final such squadron in the US Marine Corps' tactical air fleet. Based at Marine Corps Air Station Beaufort, South Carolina, the unit remains busy.

LIEUTENANT COLONEL JARROD Allen took command of VMFA(AW)-224 in the early part of 2024. At the time his command tour started, the squadron was preparing its fleet of F/A-18C and F/A-18D Hornet aircraft for a transoceanic ferry between Beaufort and Iwakuni, Japan. The trip was being made at the time that the aircraft were receiving new APG-79 AESA radars.

The APG-79(V)4 is the version installed on US Marine Corps F/A-18 Hornets. It is the first airborne GaN-AESA fire-control radar. A pre-production APG-79(V)4 radar system was successfully flown on a US Marine Corps F/A-18 Hornet in early 2022 at Naval Air Weapons Station China Lake, California. The US Marine Corps pilot demonstrated the radar's integration with the avionics of the legacy Hornet aircraft.

Discussing the squadron's transition to the new radar, Lt Col Allen said that all the

Above: **Marines with VMFA(AW)-224 conduct maintenance on F/A-18 Hornets in preparation for exercise Freezing Winds 23 at Tampere-Pirkkala Air Base, Finland.**
US Marine Corps/Cpl Adam Henke

Left: **An aircraft ordnance technician with VMFA(AW)-224 transports an AGM-84D Harpoon missile at Marine Corps Air Station Iwakuni, Japan during an ordnance loading exercise.**
US Marine Corps/Sgt Jose Angeles

MARINE ALL-WEATHER FIGHTER ATTACK SQUADRON 224

BENGALS

squadron's Hornet aircraft were fitted with the new radar before leaving Beaufort for Iwakuni. He said: "We had the opportunity to train with the APG-79 radar with MAWTS-1, our weapons school, prior to deployment. MAWTS-1 staff gave us a lot of guidance on how to use the new radar and used simulation when the squadron didn't have an aircraft equipped with the APG-79. We trained quickly through that capability."

At the time of writing, the Bengals remained deployed to Iwakuni on a standard detachment under the Unit Deployment Program (UDP). Explaining, Lt Col Allen said: "UDP is a longer-term commitment for the squadron to go to Iwakuni as a bolstering of the forward force based in the AOR. Preparing for the UDP is a little bit different to preparing for a short-term deployment somewhere because we're required by Congress to deploy with a certain training readiness and an overall capability readiness. That's all stipulated in the different publications depending on the subject."

According to the US Marine Corps: "As America's expeditionary force in readiness, the US Marine Corps constantly seeks opportunities to train and partner with allies and friends in the Pacific theater. The Unit Deployment Program has been a cost-effective way to expose US-based Marine Corps units to various training environments and maintain military partnerships throughout the Asia-Pacific region. Increased forward presence also improves the US Marine Corps' ability to respond to contingencies throughout the region. To reduce the number of unaccompanied tours and improve unit continuity, the commandant of the marine corps established the UDP in October 1977 to provide for the deployment

Left: **Marines with VMFA(AW)-224 prepare for flight operations at Naval Air Facility El Centro, California while participating in a Service Level Training Exercise.** US Marine Corps

MARINE ALL-WEATHER FIGHTER ATTACK SQUADRON 224

Above: **An aircraft electrical systems technician with VMFA(AW)-224 prepares an F/A-18C for towing at Tampere-Pirrkala Air Base, Finland.**
US Marine Corps/ Cpl Adam Henke

Right: **Aviation ordnance systems technicians with VMFA(AW)-224 load a CATM-9X onto an F/A-18 Hornet at Naval Air Station Key West, Florida during air-to-air missile proficiency training.**
US Marine Corps/ Lance Cpl Kyle Baskin

Right: **Marines with VMFA(AW)-224 conduct preflight checks on F/A-18 Hornets during flight operations at Tampere-Pirrkala Air Base, Finland.**
US Marine Corps/ Cpl Adam Henke

of units to the region for periods of approximately six months."

Describing the squadron's preparation for the UDP deployment, Lt Col Allen said: "It was like every other UDP prep that I've seen in my career. We sent detachments to Naval Air Station Key West, Florida and to Marine Corps Air Station Yuma to support the Weapons and Tactics Instructor course and Service Level Training Exercises over the ranges at Twentynine Palms, California."

According to the US Marine Corps, Service Level Training Exercises provide commanders with training opportunities to increase readiness against peer adversaries in a dynamic environment through a series of phased exercises.

Allen continued: "Then we deployed to Tampere-Pirrkala Air Base, Finland in November, and December to participate in NATO Exercise Freezing Winds, the preparation for which involved receiving and wearing the correct clothing. It ended up being an incredible deployment for training. There was a Marine Corps land component, but we didn't have much integration with them. It was more with the Finnish Air Force, and a little with the Finnish Navy. We did various mission sets. The primary objective was our integration with the Finns who had just joined NATO. They were learning how to integrate more with NATO air power, learning as they go, and we learned a lot from them."

Freezing Winds 23

Freezing Winds 23 was the first major naval exercise led by Finland as a member

MARINE ALL-WEATHER FIGHTER ATTACK SQUADRON 224

of NATO. Thirty vessels and 4,000 troops conducted a joint naval operation in the Gulf of Finland and the Archipelago Sea between November 20 and December 1. Sea forces included the Standing NATO Maritime Group 1 (SNMG1) comprising three vessels from Germany and the Netherlands, and the Standing NATO Mine Countermeasures Group 1 (SNMCMG1) comprising seven vessels from Poland, Germany, the Netherlands, and France.

US Marines assigned to Marine Rotational Force-Europe and the 2nd Marine Logistics Group, and US Navy Forces Europe took part. The exercise served as a venue to increase Finnish Navy readiness and increase United States, Finland, and NATO allies' interoperability in operational logistics, integrated fires, and amphibious operations in and around Baltic Sea littorals.

Sixteen allied aircraft flew operations over southern Finland and the northern Baltic Sea including the F/A-18 Hornets assigned to VMFA(AW)-224 and a French Atlantique 2 maritime patrol aircraft.

The Bengals had just a few weeks back at Beaufort as Lt Col Allen explained: "Once we returned from Finland, we got prepped for the UDP and left for Iwakuni in March, supported by US Air Force tanker aircraft. Once at Iwakuni, we integrated with the resident F-35B squadrons, Marine Fighter Attack Squadron 121 (VMFA-121) and VMFA-242."

Valiant Shield 2024

Seemingly ever on the move, the Bengals only spent a couple of months

Left: Marines with VMFA(AW)-224 load an AGM-84D Harpoon missile onto an F/A-18C Hornet aircraft at Marine Corps Air Station Iwakuni, Japan. US Marine Corps/Sgt Jose Angeles

Below: Marines with VMFA(AW)-224 tow an F/A-18D Hornet into a hangar at Tampere-Pirkkala Air Base, Finland during Exercise Freezing Winds 23. US Marine Corps/Cpl Adam Henke

MARINE ALL-WEATHER FIGHTER ATTACK SQUADRON 224

Above: Marines with VMFA(AW)-224 conduct preflight checks on F/A-18 Hornets during flight operations at Tampere-Pirkkala Air Base, Finland.
US Marine Corps/ Cpl Adam Henke

Right: A US Marine Corps pilot with VMFA(AW)-224 walks to the flight line for flight operations at Tampere-Pirkkala Air Base, Finland.
US Marine Corps/ Cpl Adam Henke

at Iwakuni before the squadron forward deployed to Guam for Exercise Valiant Shield 24. The deployment to Guam was completed as a part of the Aviation Training Relocation Program which exercises a fighter squadron's capabilities across diverse environments in the Indo-Pacific region. Explaining, Lt Col Allen said: "We were there with VMFA-121, conducted integrated training with the US Air Force, US Navy, and US Army, and a small element from the Japanese Air Self-Defense Force.

"The pinnacle event was the SINKEX, a sinking exercise, which involved dropping ordnance on the decommissioned Austin-class amphibious transport dock, USS *Cleveland* (LPD-7), located close to the island of Palau."

According to US Pacific Fleet: "Valiant Shield 2024 conducted a sinking exercise (SINKEX) with the environmentally clean decommissioned hulk of the Austin-class amphibious transport dock, ex-USS *Cleveland* (LPD-7) more than 40 nautical miles from land in the North Pacific Ocean.

"A SINKEX generally involves air, surface, and undersea military units conducting live-fire training against a physical target. SINKEXs give participants an opportunity to gain proficiency and confidence in their weapons and systems through realistic training that cannot be duplicated in simulators.

"Each SINKEX is conducted in strict compliance with applicable US environmental laws, regulations, and permit requirements to minimize potential harm to the environment. In addition, each SINKEX vessel undergoes a

MARINE ALL-WEATHER FIGHTER ATTACK SQUADRON 224

Left: **A pilot with VMFA(AW)-224 taxies to the flight line at Marine Corps Air Station Iwakuni, Japan.** US Marine Corps/Lance Cpl Brian Bolin

Left: **An F/A-18 Hornet aircraft with VMFA(AW)-224 prior to flight operations at Marine Corps Air Station Iwakuni, Japan.** US Marine Corps/Lance Cpl Brian Bolin

MARINE ALL-WEATHER FIGHTER ATTACK SQUADRON 224

Left: An F/A-18 Hornet aircraft with VMFA(AW)-224 at Marine Corps Air Station Iwakuni, Japan. US Marine Corps/Lance Cpl Brian Bolin

Left: Marines with VMFA(AW)-224 carry a missile offloaded from an F/A-18D Hornet aircraft at Suwon Air Base, Republic of Korea. US Marine Corps/Cpl Calah Thompson

rigorous cleaning process, in accordance with Environmental Protection Agency (EPA) standards, which includes removal of all liquid polychlorinated biphenyls (PCBs) from transformers, large capacitors, and small capacitors. Additionally, petroleum is cleaned from the vessel's tanks, pipes and reservoirs and all trash, floatable materials, mercury, or fluorocarbon-containing materials, and readily detachable solid PCB items are removed. The navy also complies with documentation requirements to track components containing liquid PCBs and solid shipboard materials potentially containing PCBs.

"SINKEXs are conducted only after the area has been surveyed for the presence of people, marine vessels, aircraft, and marine species. SINKEXs are fully compliant with the National Environmental Policy Act, Marine Mammal Protection Act, Endangered Species Act, and a general permit under the Marine Protection, Research, and Sanctuaries Act.

"Valiant Shield is a multinational, biennial field training exercise focused on integrating interoperability in a multi-domain environment. The exercise builds real-world proficiency in sustaining joint forces by detecting, locating, tracking, and engaging units at sea, in the air, in space, on land, and in cyberspace in response to a range of mission areas.

"Exercises such as Valiant Shield 2024 allow forces across the Indo-Pacific the opportunity to integrate US Navy, US Marine Corps, US Army, US Air Force, US Coast Guard, US Space Force, and partner nations to train in precise, lethal, and overwhelming multi-axis, multi-domain effects that demonstrate the strength and versatility of the Joint and Combined Force."

Describing additional training at Anderson, Lt Col Allen said: "We were at Anderson for six weeks as a squadron. Exercise Valiant Shield lasted for two weeks when the squadron undertook

Below: An F/A-18C Hornet aircraft with VMFA(AW)-224 takes off from Andersen Air Force Base, Guam during training as part of the Aviation Training Relocation programme to enhance interservice capabilities and to sustain high operational readiness in the Indo-Pacific. US Marine Corps/Sgt Jose Angeles

MARINE ALL-WEATHER FIGHTER ATTACK SQUADRON 224

Above: **An F/A-18C Hornet aircraft with VMFA(AW)-224 taxies to the flight line at Andersen Air Force Base, Guam.** US Marine Corps/Sgt Jose Angeles

Left: **Marines with VMFA(AW)-224 offload a missile from an F/A-18D Hornet aircraft at Suwon Air Base, Republic of Korea.** US Marine Corps/Cpl Calah Thompson

Below: **A pilot with VMFA(AW)-224 prepares for flight operations at Marine Corps Air Station Iwakuni, Japan.** US Marine Corps/Lance Cpl Brian Bolin

cruise missile defense and defensive counter air, some aerial interdiction missions, and shot five AGM-88 HARM missiles. Independent of the exercise, we also dropped AGM-154 Joint Stand-Off Weapon, a variety of other high explosive bombs, and rockets for unit level training. All missions were flown over the water."

According to the US Navy: "The JSOW family consists of multiple weapon variants. The AGM-154A configuration is used to attack fixed and relocatable soft targets such as parked aircraft, trucks, armored personnel carriers, and surface-to-air missile sites. A modified version, the AGM-154A-1, includes a BLU-111 warhead. The AGM-154C variant incorporates a 500-pound blast/fragmentation/penetrator warhead effective against fixed-point targets such as industrial facilities, logistical systems, and hardened tactical targets. This variant uses an uncooled, long-wave imaging infrared seeker with autonomous target acquisition for precise targeting. The latest variant, the JSOW C-1, is the navy's first air-to-ground, network-enabled weapon capable of attacking stationary land and moving maritime targets. It includes GPS/INS guidance, terminal IR seeker and a Link-16 weapon data link."

Lt Col Allen described the employment of weapons as, "a good opportunity for our ordnance marines to load munitions and to see it get employed, and for a lot of our aircrew to drop ordnance for the first time in their career.

"At the end of the six-week TDY we returned to Iwakuni for about a month and then flew to Suwon Air Base in the Republic of Korea flying missions with the RoKAF's 10th Fighter Wing. We're the first marine unit to come here for a detachment.

"Since May 2024, we've substantially ramped-up our flight operations and completed more training opportunities and missions. At the end of the Suwon-based det, the squadron will return to Iwakuni and pick up UDP. Once we return to Beaufort, the one event we're tasked for is to support the WTI course in the spring of 2025. Following that, during the summer of 2025 we will start the squadron's transition to the F-35."

THE ACE OF SPADES

Marine Attack Squadron 231 (VMA-231) 'Ace of Spades' is the last but one frontline, east coast AV-8B Harrier squadron in the 2nd Marine Aircraft Wing.

MAJOR JASON GRENIER has served with VMA-231 since the third quarter of 2019. He became a weapons and tactics instructor in 2023 after graduating from the WTI course with Marine Aviation Weapons and Tactics Squadron 1 (MAWTS-1) based at Marine Corps Air Station Yuma, Arizona.

Discussing VMA-231 flight operations from Cherry Point, Maj Grenier said: "Cherry Point's location is central to a lot of east coast-based units: US Marine Corps, US Navy, or US Air Force, so VMA-231 is able to practice with different units in the different ranges. We routinely go on detachments for training to other parts of the country. Sometimes we partner with units that were unfamiliar with, in areas that we're not used to."

VMA-231's mission essential tasks (METs) include close air support which involves working with a JTAC, a Joint Terminal Air Controller to direct fire support for marines located on a range somewhere. Strike missions can involve dropping inert or live ordnance as Maj Grenier explained: "Different ranges have different regulations, but a couple allow us, most of the time, to simulate dropping ordnance, just because it's easier to do, and doesn't require certain range restrictions which are in place when you are delivering [real] ordnance. Another range permits us to deliver ordnance, and we've done several training events involving dropping real inert ordnance in some kind of strike profile."

Explaining training for SCAR (Strike Co-ordination and Reconnaissance), the major said: "SCAR is undertaken in pretty much the same way as a strike mission. We usually practice SCAR in house, or we'll pair up with an HMLA unit based at New River to complete training events on the local ranges.

"Day-to-day flying is spent maintaining proficiency in our core METS but to conduct those essential missions and grease the squadron's ability to move assets and get used to doing that, we regularly deploy to California and Florida on DFTs or detachments for training. DFTs help maintain the expeditionary feel of the Marine Corps and involve calling upon

Above: **AV-8B Harriers conduct an aerial refuel off the coast of Louisiana. The aircraft are assigned to VMA-231.** US Marine Corps/Cpl Cody Rowe

MARINE ATTACK SQUADRON 231

Above: AV-8B Harriers assigned to VMA-231 conduct aerial refuelling during an exercise to enhance the squadron's air-to-air and air-to-ground capabilities.
US Marine Corps/Cpl Cody Rowe

Right: US Marine Corps/Cpl Cody Rowe

and coordinating the logistics, ordnance, and aviation aspects so people don't forget how to do that.

"At Twentynine Palms, California we undertake exercises with HMLA squadrons, F/A-18 squadrons, and ground units. It's a good training area for different squadrons to operate together and practice MAGTF operations. Operating at Twentynine Palms makes such a difference from dropping bombs on a field in the middle of nowhere, to dropping bombs on a target close to marines on the ground, which is a process all Harrier pilots must practice and get used to.

Right: US Marine Corps/Cpl Christian Cortez

MARINE ATTACK SQUADRON 231

Right: **An AV-8B Harrier assigned to VMA-231, vertically lands on the flight deck of the amphibious assault ship USS *Kearsarge* (LHD 3) during carrier qualifications.** US Marine Corps/ Cpl Christian Cortez

Right: **The pilot of an AV-8B Harrier assigned to VMA-231 receives the signal for take-off from the flight deck of the amphibious assault ship USS *Kearsarge* (LHD 3) during carrier qualifications prior to deployment with the 26th Marine Expeditionary Unit.** US Marine Corps/Cpl Christian Cortez

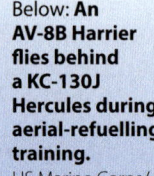

Below: **An AV-8B Harrier flies behind a KC-130J Hercules during aerial-refuelling training.** US Marine Corps/ SSgt Theodore Bergan

"The Weapons and Tactics Instructor course run by MAWTS-1 at Yuma is a very good aviation-based training experience. During the past 12 months, VMA-231 has sent personnel to both Twentynine Palms and WTI but has not sent any Harrier aircraft.

"We recently supported an event called Distributed Aviation Operations Exercise 24 [DAOEx 24], which was designed to distribute the command and control of aviation forces across echelons of command, and to push authorities to the lowest levels, while keeping forces moving between airfields and air sites. Logistically, the exercise proved to be good practice to move a large organisation around the country."

VMA-231 and Marine Fighter Attack Squadron 312 (VMFA-312) deployed to Cecil Airport, Florida and flew a mix of air-to-air and air-to-ground missions in DAOEx 24. Marine Light Attack Helicopter Squadron 167 (HMLA-167) participated in DAOEx 24 at the US Navy Atlantic Undersea Test and Evaluation Center on Andros Island, Bahamas.

VMA-231 expects to return to Twentynine Palms to support training events this year and will deploy to Nellis Air Force Base in support of USAF training. VMA-231 will then slowly wind down its operations to its Harrier sunset and prepare for transition to the F-35B at Cherry Point which is planned to begin in FY2026.

Marine Expeditionary Unit

An element from VMA-231 returned to Cherry Point on March 16, 2024 from the USS *Bataan* (LHD 5) after an eight-month deployment, marking the end of

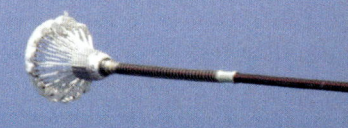

MARINE ATTACK SQUADRON 231

Left: US Marine Corps/SSgt Theodore Bergan

The 26th MEU(SOC) serves as one of America's premier crisis response forces capable of conducting amphibious operations and limited contingency operations, to include enabling the introductions of follow-on forces and designated special operations, in support of theatre requirements of the geographic combatant commander.

Outlining the remaining time for VMA-231 to operate the Harrier, Maj Grenier said: "We have over a year remaining as a Harrier squadron before we start the transition to the F-35B. That will be a lengthy process once 231 stops flying the Harrier. Both VMA-231 and VMA-223 'Bulldogs' (the final US Marine Corps Harrier squadron) will transition to the F-35B at Cherry Point. I'm due to train on the F-35B this year, which I'm looking forward to."

Weapons and Tactic Instructor Course

Maj Grenier completed the US Marine Corps Weapons and Tactics Instructor course in late 2023. Describing the aircraft's inclusion, he said: "Harriers are usually and primarily given strike type missions in WTI, which as a training course affords more assets to operate with than you usually have in other exercises.

"One night-time WTI sortie involved flying at low altitude using NVGs to avoid hitting the ground. It was a very satisfying mission, and I've never had the opportunity to do that anywhere else.

"The large mission flown at the end of the course was complex. It wasn't necessarily the problem solving you had to go through but understanding all the capabilities of the different weapon systems' capabilities, what those platforms could do well, and being able to take that into account.

"Usually, you don't have the opportunity to integrate with that many people. It's very easy to plan a mission, but when you're out on a mission with different

the squadron's final Harrier deployment with a Marine Expeditionary Unit prior to transition to F-35Bs.

The VMA-231 element was assigned to the 26th Marine Expeditionary Unit (Special Operations Capable) which served as the Tri-Geographic Combatant Command crisis response force. The deployment marked the first time a MEU with the Special Operations Capable (SOC) designation had been employed in over two decades. While deployed, more than 4,000 Marines and sailors supported a wide range of interoperability training, exercises and operations within the US 5th and 6th Fleet areas of operations covering the High North, Baltic Sea, Eastern Mediterranean, Arabian Gulf, Red Sea, and Middle East.

More specifically, the 26th MEU(SOC) supported operations and engagements, conducted theatre security cooperation activities, bilateral training with NATO allies and partners, and executed sustainment training to ensure the force was ready and postured to respond to any crisis in the region.

Below: **Marines with VMA-231 prepare to tow an AV-8B Harrier at Naval Air Station Joint Reserve Base New Orleans, Louisiana, during Exercise Southern Strike 2023. The joint, multinational exercise is designed to improve interoperability among allies and branches of the Department of Defense.** US Marine Corps/Cpl Christian Cortez

US NAVY AND MARINE CORPS YEARBOOK **2024**

MARINE ATTACK SQUADRON 231

assets that bring their capabilities to the fight, you plan for all the contingencies. In my opinion, WTI brought all the assets together very well and gave you a general baseline knowledge of how different systems work and how they execute their roles.

During my WTI course, we flew some large force exercises integrating with F-35s which undertook most of the heavy lifting in those events. Integrating with the F-35 gives the Harrier the opportunity to work in environments that it wouldn't be able to do by itself. The Harrier is effective at a lot of different missions but whenever F-35s are in the area we usually have a better chance of success in what we are trying to do."

Key West DFT

During its DFT, a lot of the missions flown by VMA-231 pilots from Naval Air Station Key West were core METs. Maj Grenier said: "We did a lot of CAS over the range with JTACs to work through different CAS scenarios. A benefit of going to Key West is to practice logistics movement and to feel uncomfortable with being in different airspace. It's easy to do CAS on the ranges near Cherry Point, and when you've done that a hundred times it feels very familiar. The challenge is whether you still do CAS when you're in a new area? The hairs on the back of your neck stand-up because you're not entirely comfortable, so it's

Right: **Pilots of US Marine Corps tactical aircraft such as the AV-8B Harrier regularly conduct aerial-refuelling training to maximise proficiency in the procedure.** US Marine Corps/SSgt Theodore Bergan

Right: **Marines with VMA-231 remove the engine from an AV-8B Harrier.** US Marine Corps/Cpl Christian Cortez

Below: **An aircraft airframes mechanic with VMA-231 operates a crane to remove the wing assembly from an AV-8B Harrier at Naval Air Station Joint Reserve Base New Orleans, Louisiana.** US Marine Corps/Cpl Christian Cortez

MARINE ATTACK SQUADRON 231

Right: **A pilot with VMA-231 performs pre-flight checks in an AV-8B Harrier prior to a mission from Naval Air Station Joint Reserve Base New Orleans, Louisiana, during Exercise Southern Strike 2023.** US Marine Corps/Cpl Christian Cortez

Right: US Marine Corps/Cpl Christian Cortez

Below left: **An aircraft mechanic with VMA-231 signals to the pilot prior to take-off.** US Marine Corps/Cpl Christian Cortez

Below right: US Marine Corps/Cpl Aziza Kamuhanda

US NAVY AND MARINE CORPS YEARBOOK 2024

MARINE ATTACK SQUADRON 231

Left: **An AV-8B Harrier assigned to Marine Attack Squadron 231 Detachment, Marine Medium Tiltrotor Squadron 162 (Reinforced), 26th Marine Expeditionary Unit (Special Operations Capable) lands at Marine Corps Air Station Cherry Point, North Carolina, on March 16, 2024. The force had just completed an eight-month deployment embarked aboard the amphibious assault ship USS** *Bataan* **(LHD 5).**
US Marine Corps/Cpl Aziza Kamuhanda

good to practice that. Similarly, we did some SCAR and strike missions."

Harrier Configuration

VMA-231's Harrier aircraft are currently operating with the latest mission software known as Operational Flight Program 7.1 (OFP 7.1). Follow-on OFPs are currently in development but given the time remaining until the Harrier's retirement, it remains to be seen if either will be released to the fleet.

OFP 7.1 supports the carriage and employment of the Block II AIM-9X Sidewinder air-to-air missile, which is currently in testing and Major Grenier is not aware whether the missile will be implemented on the Harrier.

According to the FY2023 annual report by the Director, Operational Test and Evaluation: "The AIM-9X Block II is the latest generation, infrared, short-range, air-intercept missile designed to detect, acquire, intercept, and destroy a wide range of airborne threats. It is day and night capable, uses a passive infrared seeker, and is capable of large attack angles against a wide variety of enemy aircraft. The designated threshold platforms are the F/A-18C/D Hornet and F/A-18E/F Super Hornet, and the F-15C/D Eagle. Current and future integration efforts also include the AV-8B."

Similarly, a couple of data link systems are also in development. Such add-ons are introduced as the Harrier gains the latest OFP update, but the TTNT remains in development to achieve full functionality.

Left: **The pilot of an AV-8B Harrier lands during field carrier-landing practice at Marine Corps Auxiliary Landing Field Bogue, North Carolina.**
US Marine Corps/LCpl Orlanys Diaz Figueroa

Below: **An AV-8B Harrier taxies at Marine Corps Air Station Cherry Point, North Carolina.**
US Marine Corps/LCpl Orlanys Diaz Figueroa

MARINE ATTACK SQUADRON 231

Left: **A Marine Attack Squadron 231 Detachment, Marine Medium Tiltrotor Squadron 162 (Reinforced), 26th Marine Expeditionary Unit (Special Operations Capable) returned to Marine Corps Air Station Cherry Point, North Carolina, on March 16, 2024, following an eight-month deployment aboard the amphibious assault ship USS *Bataan* (LHD 5).** US Marine Corps/Cpl Aziza Kamuhanda

In 2022, the AGM-158 JASSM stand-off missile was being touted for integration on the Harrier, but with the aircraft's retirement just around the corner, the test timeline for its integration and introduction to the fleet has been delayed.

One improvement that has made it to the Harrier fleet is the wing tip station upgrade, one that enables the aircraft to carry air-to-air missiles on its wing tip stations.

Flying the Harrier

Describing what the Harrier is like to fly, Maj Grenier said: "When you first learn to fly the Harrier, it gives you that feeling from when you first learned how to drive. Your parents allowed you on the highway, and you made it out alive. It felt uncomfortable, but you did it, then you got used to it, and got more comfortable.

"When you've returned to your parking spot in a Harrier, you're very dirty because there's grease all over the place. But is does the tasks we ask it to do, and it does them very well.

"Usually when we're in the area and people want to do CAS, they usually ask for Harriers, because we practice CAS a lot. Ergonomically the controls for the HOTAS, targeting pod and systems are set-up very well for CAS. The big canopy allows you to easily see out and you have room to manoeuvre in the cockpit.

"When it comes to dropping a bomb on a target, you can do it very quickly and very reactively, it takes three button pushes. Other aircraft require more button pushes and use a different logic for dropping a bomb.

"The Harrier is very hands on. As a Harrier pilot you get to do a lot of very interesting flying, a lot of weapons drops, and a lot of low-level flying, which from a pilot's perspective is very satisfying. Then you have the F-35B which is the new toy with all the bells and whistles, which takes some of the stick and rudder away from the pilot and allows the computer to do that. While it's a very capable aircraft, it doesn't have the gritty fun character of the Harrier, which I'll kind of miss.

"The British used the Harrier in different scenarios during the Falklands war and you did it well. It was a very interesting plane that the British created, and it's fun and notable for us to bring the aircraft to its end in service with the US Marine Corps."

Left: US Marine Corps/LCpl Orlanys Diaz Figueroa

Left: **Marines assigned to Marine Attack Squadron 231 Detachment, Marine Medium Tiltrotor Squadron 162 (Reinforced), 26th Marine Expeditionary Unit (Special Operations Capable) prepare to disembark an AV-8B Harrier after returning from deployment at Marine Corps Air Station Cherry Point, North Carolina, on March 16, 2024.** US Marine Corps/Cpl Aziza Kamuhanda

MARINE LIGHT ATTACK HELICOPTER TRAINING SQUADRON 303

AH-1Z AND UH-1Y TRAINING

Marine Light Attack Helicopter Training Squadron 303 (HMLAT-303) 'Atlas' is the only H-1 training squadron in the US Marine Corps. Its home station is Marine Corps Air Station Camp Pendleton, California.

MARINE LIGHT ATTACK Helicopter Training Squadron (HMLAT) -303 has a straightforward mission: to conduct an extensive training syllabus on the AH-Z and UH-1Y helicopters to include familiarisation, navigation, ordnance, formation, night-vision goggle use, terrain, and instrument training. The squadron also provides introductory and some advanced level maintenance training.

HMLAT-303 is the largest HMLA squadron in terms of aircraft and the number of hours flown each year, in FY2023 the squadron flew about 6,700 hours. Production is about 70 pilots (40 Cobra and 30 Huey) and 45 crew chiefs a year. Most of the squadron's flight operations are flown locally at Camp Pendleton, which occupies approximately 125,000 acres of land which include ranges suitable for H-1 training.

Explaining, Lieutenant Colonel Jason Caster, HMLAT-303's commanding officer said: "The bulk of flying is familiarisation which is done locally on the Camp Pendleton range complex. Generally, we take off, fly to the beach line, land on one of the pads out there, work on profiles, or we fly to a couple of outlying fields to the north of the range and practice landing so we're not clogging up the tower pattern. Specific weapons delivery is also done on using a low impact area of the range twice a week. We do go over the hill and use some of the ranges near El Centro.

"Navigation, instrument flying, formation flying all involve departing Camp Pendleton, to force the student to navigate in and around some of the complex airspaces that exist in southern California and utilising the ranges and then return to base.

"We use different types of pads: LHD (a Wasp-class amphibious assault ship), LSD (dock landing ship), or LPD (amphibious transport dock), each has the markings of the relevant type of amphibious ship. We use the LHD pad because it's a longer concrete area, suited to introductory training and a lot of low work. Operational squadrons use the LHD pad for field carrier landing practice (FCLPs). Two other pads are set out to represent the landing deck of an LSD or an LPD.

"Some of the pads are located near the beach. The beach is unique and affects a pilot's sight picture, the cliffs make it challenging, especially at night when students struggle and show what their weaknesses are. Then we fly back inland and land at places that have a little bit more texture where they usually improve."

Some training is undertaken away from Pendleton as HMLAT-303's commanding officer, Lieutenant Colonel Jason Caster explained: "We conduct detachments to Havasu City Municipal Airport in Arizona and Naval Air Facility El Centro in California, but we also try to det to

Below: **An AH-1Z assigned to Marine Light Attack Training Squadron 303 (HMLAT-303) based at Camp Pendleton hovers over the flight line.**
US Marine Corps/ LCpl Jaime Reyes

MARINE LIGHT ATTACK HELICOPTER TRAINING SQUADRON 303

unfamiliar locations to expose our personnel, primarily the maintainers, to doing the logistic and maintenance planning. For example, in April, we sent two Cobras and two Hueys to participate in an air show in Canada. That was a 2,600-mile cross country which we completed on time there and back. It was a different event for a fleet replacement squadron and one that operational squadrons train to execute.

"Most of our training doesn't qualify as exercise or even tactical level. It is very much the basic level, five to six stages, depending on the platform, learning how to fly the aircraft, take-offs, landings, and flying different foundational profiles. Then you complete an introduction to weapons delivery, the focus is on the different ways you can employ rockets and guns, and for the Cobra employment of precision-guided munitions and the AGR-20 Advanced Precision Kill Weapon System.

"You also train in navigation, instruments, TERF, which is terrain flying at low-altitudes, all at the introductory level during both day and night conditions. When a student joins their fleet squadron they start with what we label 2000 level training, which involves flying in tactical scenarios and participation in exercises.

"In accordance with the 303's curriculum, students do not have a requirement to fly with any other types in the MAGTF, they just need to know how to safely employ the aircraft when they leave 303, because they will subsequently fly in exercises and operations with a senior instructor who is

Above: Marines with HMLAT-303 clean an AH-1Z helicopter. US Marine Corps/ LCpl Jaime Reyes

Left: A marine with HMLAT-303 hoses down an AH-1Z helicopter at Marine Corps Air Station Camp Pendleton. US Marine Corps/ LCpl Jaime Reyes

Below: US Marine Corps/LCpl Jaime Reyes

MARINE LIGHT ATTACK HELICOPTER TRAINING SQUADRON 303

going to provide additional tactical training as they do the remainder of the syllabus."

Explaining the different phases of training undertaken by H-1 pilots from the time they start with HMLAT-303, Lt Col Caster said: "The Training and Readiness (T&R) manual lays out all training events in the H-1 syllabus which is driven directly by the mission essential tasks (METs) assigned to an operational HMLA."

Training Phases

Training and Readiness comprises six phases (levels) of training:

1000 Level, introductory core skills, foundational to safety of flight.
2000 Level, core skills, foundational to effective execution.
3000 Level, mission skills, foundational to tactical execution.
4000 Level, core plus skills, advanced/exquisite skill sets.
4000 Level, mission plus skills, advanced or higher threat mission sets.
5000 Level, Instructor training.
6000 Level, qualification, and designation training.

Bottom: **A UH-1Y lifts off from a parking spot on HMLAT-303's extensive flight line at Marine Corps Air Station Camp Pendleton.**
US Marine Corps/LCpl Jaime Reyes

Below: **A marine with Marine Light Attack Training Squadron 303 (HMLAT-303) signals to the pilot of a UH-1Y to remain in the hover on a flight line parking spot at Marine Corps Air Station Camp Pendleton.**
US Marine Corps/LCpl Jaime Reyes

The HMLAT-303 boss said: "Core skills are related to aircraft capability and limitations while mission skills are related to tactical capability and execution. Core skills are the foundational blocking and tackling that are applied for safe and effective flight operations. Mission skills are about choosing the right core skills to use for the tactical situation and are focused on combat training.

"Each phase has a specific level of training with individual stages tied to skills or METs. An example, a 2600 is a specific weapons delivery event that allows effective execution of a 3300 close air support event. The 3300 focus is on the correct application of specific weapon delivery profiles for the threat on the battlefield. Both build on each other and provide readiness to the close air support MET.

"A typical timeline for an H-1 pilot starts with their orders to HMLAT-303, the fleet replacement squadron (FRS). The timeline is not completely sequential but training at each phase generally occurs in the windows listed below with a first fleet tour having a typical length of 48 months.

"Introductory core skills are completed at HMLAT-303 from 0-6 months. Core skills are completed at an operational HMLA from 6-18 months. Mission skills are completed at an operational HMLA

MARINE LIGHT ATTACK HELICOPTER TRAINING SQUADRON 303

Left: **A UH-1Y assigned to HMLAT-303 with its rotors turning prior to hover taxi for take-off from Marine Corps Air Station Camp Pendleton.**
US Marine Corps/ LCpl Jaime Reyes

from 10-39 months. Core/mission plus skills are completed at operational HMLA from 13-48 months. Instructor training is completed at operational HMLA from 30-48 months. Qualification and designation training are completed at an operational HMLA from 6-48 months.

"AH-1 and UH-1 training is very similar because most of the METs are executed by both platforms with five core METs being trained to by both platforms. The AH-1 has six core METs (one dissimilar from the UH-1) and three core plus METs (two dissimilar). The UH-1 has seven core METs (two dissimilar) and five core plus METs (four dissimilar). The dissimilarities come from each platform's specific design capabilities and limitations. The training syllabi are very much integrated with operational HMLAs often using mixed platform flights (two or more aircraft) to leverage those dissimilarities.

"Cobra and Huey pilots do not generally fly together at 303 because the respective T&R manuals are slightly misaligned as the Huey has a couple of extra mission sets. As a utility aircraft, Huey pilots have additional training focussed on assault support. The Cobras have more weapons specific training, so the syllabi don't always line up.

"The profiles we teach are all designed around applicability to different operating environments including traditional and non-traditional amphibious ships as well as shore-based sites, distributed maritime operations, and expeditionary advanced base operations.

A helicopter can be flown safely using a number of varying profiles depending on your style and preference, but the standardised profiles and the way we teach them are designed to provide a precision type approach that you can apply to landing on the runway numbers, for a confined area landing site, or for landing on multiple types of ships, because the requirement from a helicopter standpoint is to put the skids down where you intended. If the landing spot happens to be moving and over the water, it doesn't change the way that you fly the profile. It just changes how you set up.

"Our teaching gets them comfortable with the foundations of flying the aircraft, so that they can very quickly transition into tactical flight operations. Carrier qualifications are substantial for the H-1 community and are training to and executed in the fleet HMLA. You do day and night FCLPs to a concrete deck that is appropriately marked for the ship you are training to land on. Once you've done those, you execute one day, one night and one night unaided landing evolution to the ship. Then you're qualified and proficient to land on a ship deck during operations. Landing on a ship is a core plus skill and required for readiness when you are expected to deploy or execute operations from a ship"

The US Marine Corps' Force Design 2030 concept of operation has not changed HMLAT-303's introductory training curriculum because the course is foundational and the METs are tied to the capability of the aircraft."

Explaining, Lt Col Caster said: "When we next review our assigned METs, we'll start to incorporate some new force design driven METs into the training syllabus, but

Below: **Marines with Marine Light Attack Training Squadron 303 (HMLAT-303) run through pre-flight checks before engine start for a mission from Camp Pendleton.**
US Marine Corps/ LCpl Jaime Reyes

US NAVY AND MARINE CORPS YEARBOOK 2024

MARINE LIGHT ATTACK HELICOPTER TRAINING SQUADRON 303

Left: A marine assigned to HMLAT-303 checks an engine component during maintenance on a UH-1Y AT Marine Corps Air Station Camp Pendleton.
US Marine Corps/LCpl Jaime Reyes

Left: US Marine Corps/LCpl Juan Anaya

Below: Marines with Marine Light Attack Helicopter Training Squadron 303 (HMLAT-303) load rockets into the rocket pod on a UH-1Y helicopter at Marine Corps Air Station Camp Pendleton.
US Marine Corps/Cpl Dylan Chagnon

training to those new METs will likely occur at the fleet HMLA squadrons, not at 303. That's because the new systems coming down the line for H-1s will be introduced to the operational HMLA squadrons first. 303 may introduce some of these systems in the simulator for exposure to the new METs. It is important for the H-1 to continue to integrate systems that increase our precision-guided munition capability and survivability. H-1 aircraft truly tied into the digital network enabling quick transmission of information across platforms provides significant capability to the ground force commander."

Training Devices

Detailing the latest types of training devices used by HMLAT-303, Lt Col Caster said: "The Marine Corps has begun using the Marine Common Aircrew Trainer (MCAT), a simulator that can be configured for H-1s, H-53s and V-22s which is set-up with a full cabin and weapon systems. We recently formalised the incorporation of MCAT into the UH-1Y aircrew T&R manual.

"Many of our introductory events in the T&R use an MCAT. Events such as the weapons checklist, weapons handling, and the procedures and actions undertaken in the aft cabin for the assault support role, providing tactical mobility and logistic support to the MAGTF for the movement of high priority personnel and cargo within the immediate area

MARINE LIGHT ATTACK HELICOPTER TRAINING SQUADRON 303

of operations, or the evacuation of personnel and cargo.

"MCAT provides a safe environment in which aircrew can get lots of reps, while learning how to man the gun and make all their calls. We find the MCAT to be super useful, the system has really improved the quality of exposure for our aircrew to events only encountered during live fire events, so the aircrew's familiarity with the weapon systems has increased."

According to Naval Air Systems Command's PMA-205: "A Marine Common Aircrew Trainer or MCAT is used to conduct initial, integrated crew training and proficiency flights, ultimately reducing flight hours in operational aircraft, reducing and in some cases eliminating ordnance expenditures, and reducing high-risk evolutions that could lead to mishaps. The fleet began training in the MCAT in the spring of 2022.

"Prior to the delivery of the new device, Marine Corps CH-53E, MV-22B, and UH-1Y enlisted aircrew trained on operational aircraft. The new system enables non-pilot aircrew to maintain and enhance individual and unit mission readiness and will allow the marine corps to optimise aircraft flight hour utilisation by offering a new, state-of-the-art, simulation-based alternative."

Captain Lisa Sullivan, then programme manager for Naval Aviation Training Systems and Ranges Program Office PMA-205 programme manager said: "In the past, H-60, H-53, H-1, and V-22 aircrew did not have an opportunity to start their training in a controlled simulator environment before entering a dynamic aircraft environment. For our Marine Corps aircrew, it provides the ability to gain initial weapon engagement proficiency in a simulator before live-fire training on operational flights."

Another training device called the H-1 mission rehearsal trainer (MRT) was introduced at Pendleton in the spring of 2023 and is expected to be fielded with each Marine Aircraft Group next year.

Commenting on the mission rehearsal trainer, Lt Col Caster said: "The MRT probably won't be completely

Right: **A marine aircraft ordnance technician with HMLAT-303 loads a training round rocket into the pod on a UH-1Y helicopter during an aircraft ordnance load at Marine Corps Air Station Camp Pendleton.** US Marine Corps/Cpl Dylan Chagnon

Right: **A UH-1Y assigned to Marine Light Helicopter Attack Training Squadron 303 lifts an aging water guzzler from Harper Canyon located in Anza-Borrego Desert State Park, California.** US Marine Corps/Chief Warrant Officer 2 Trent Randolph

Left: **A marine loads ammunition onto a UH-1Y helicopter during an aircraft ordnance load at Marine Corps Air Station Camp Pendleton, California. Ordnance loads are conducted regularly to support the required weapon qualifications and training of aircraft crew members and crew chiefs on the various ranges aboard Marine Corps Base Camp Pendleton.** US Marine Corps/Cpl Dylan Chagnon

MARINE LIGHT ATTACK HELICOPTER TRAINING SQUADRON 303

applicable to 303's mission in terms of the effectiveness of, for example, the flight controls, for foundational learning. At 303 we introduce students to the basics of flying a new aircraft and try to prepare them for the fleet, which means learning how to think as part of a combat crew. The basics of flying the aircraft are foundational but a secondary training objective is to develop a dynamic thought mindset about what you're doing to increase the effectiveness of the mission.

"Holistically across the fleet, the mission rehearsal trainer will allow aircrew to rehearse missions and get better at the things that are new to them. Stick skills aren't completely new to them, but absorb a lot of their mental capacity when they're flying a new aircraft. What is new in H-1 training is the way that we think about how to fly an aircraft compared to how it's flown at flight school. So anytime they can rehearse it will make them much better."

An interesting fact about the H-1 helicopter is that they are flown single piloted, but a pilot never flies solo.

Above: **A UH-1Y helicopter assigned to HMLAT-303 takes off after inserting a ground control team at Anza-Borrego Desert State Park, California to assist with lifting water guzzlers to locations throughout the park. Guzzlers are self-filling, constructed watering facilities that collect, store, and make water available for wildlife.** US Marine Corps/Chief Warrant Officer 2 Trent Randolph

Left: **A marine gives a salute to the pilot of a UH-1Y helicopter as he lifts from a parking spot at Camp Pendleton.** US Marine Corps/LCpl Joshua Young

MARINE LIGHT ATTACK HELICOPTER TRAINING SQUADRON 303

Above: A UH-1Y assigned to HMLAT-303 lifts from a tactical aircraft landing area at Camp Pendleton. US Marine Corps/ LCpl Maritza Vela

"When a student pilot starts flight operations at 303, they will fly with as many different instructors as is possible, to increase their experience level, but also to increase, what we refer to as their tool bag of different techniques based on each instructor's variation in the way that they apply the foundational skills. The HMLAT-303 staff tries to keep students in each class progressing at the same rate, so they start the syllabus at the same time and can help each other in planning."

Crew Chiefs

Crew chiefs are the responsibility of a crew member training team which takes them through the syllabus – academics and training flights. The team pair-up two or four student crew chiefs as a group for the duration of the syllabus, so they all prepare for the same events. The team rotates instructors through the groups so that each instructor gets a better look at each student. Consequently, all instructors can discuss the strengths and weaknesses of each student, and then try to find the optimum training environment to get a student to be as effective as possible.

Kinetic Events

Students training on the Cobra and the Huey learn to fire kinetic weapons as part of the course. Explaining, Lt Col Caster said: "It's probably one of the most impactful events for a student because that's when

Discussing the situation, Lt Col Caster said: "When a student pilot graduates from the 303 course, they are NATOPS qualified. They can legally take an aircraft and fly around doing a familiarisation mission set or ferry the aircraft somewhere, but they do not have proficiency in the tactical skills at that point. When a student gets to a fleet HMLA squadron, they become a aircraft commander in training and execute tactical operations as a copilot. That's governed by how our readiness is designed. A senior instructor, such as the squadron Weapons and Tactics Instructor (WTI), compensates for an individual without a qualification so that when you pair them together as pilot and copilot, you have a crew able to execute the assigned mission..

"Subsequently throughout your career, as you grow into an instructor role you will start to fly with more junior individuals. Generally, you spend the smallest amount of time in your career flying with a pilot or copilot that has the same qualifications you do. There is almost always an instructor and student dynamic to the crew pairing.

"There is no traditional solo flight in the 303 course like you would get in some single-piloted aircraft when you transition from flying with an instructor to now flying by yourself. This is because of the requirement to have both crew seats filled.

Right: Two UH-1Ys, one AH-1W Super Cobra and one AH-1Z hover several hundred yards away from their target during an aerial demonstration at Marine Corps Base Camp Pendleton. During the demonstration, marines on the ground communicated with the helicopters to perform a multi-phase, live-fire event. US Marine Corps/Sgt Lillian Stephens

MARINE LIGHT ATTACK HELICOPTER TRAINING SQUADRON 303

Right: **Marines and Czech Air Force airmen assigned to HMLAT-303 hover taxi to the runway at Marine Corps Air Station Camp Pendleton during a training course for the Czech personnel. The Czech Republic has purchased AH-1Z and UH-1Y helicopters via a US government Foreign Military Sale.** US Marine Corps/ Sgt Rachaelanne Woodward

Below left: **A crew chief looks out at a second UH-1Y during a demonstration of the tactical capabilities and combat power of the H-1 platform.** US Marine Corps/Cpl Sarah Marshall

Below right: **A crew chief looks out at a formation of AH-1Z and UH-1T helicopters during a combat power demonstration at Camp Pendleton.** US Marine Corps/Cpl Sarah Marshall

you start to realize your mission as a combat pilot is more than just flying. I can still remember my first weapons delivery flight at 303. I was sitting in the left seat, and the 0.50 Cal went off next to my ear, and it made me jump, and it happens to every student that does it, so it's a good exposure event for them. It also introduces the important of effective and accurate fires because someone on the ground is counting on you to hit what you are aiming at."

"A Cobra pilot completes two firing events, one from the front seat, and one in the back seat, a Huey pilot also flies two such firing events. Students fly both a lower altitude ingress and a higher altitude ingress, simulating either medium or low threat environments while focusing the student's training on ballistic weapons; shooting rockets and the guns at a big rock on the side of a hill. It teaches them how to get into that profile, get the nose pointed in the right direction, and then get out of that profile without hitting the ground. Almost everything that they go on to do in the fleet incorporates those profiles in some capacity or another, especially for the Cobra; that's all that thing is designed to do!"

Type Selection

So how does a young pilot graduating their flying training course know which type of H-1 they will fly? Explaining, Lt Col Caster said: "Naval Training Command projects a certain number of student pilots for each type, whether that's Cobra or Huey. As students graduate from their course with Training Air Wing 5 at Naval Air Station Whiting Field, Florida, the wing conducts graduation drafts, from which each graduate is selected for a specific pipeline. Each student submits a wish list when they graduate listing in order of platform preference and which coast they would like and the combinations thereof. Consequently, each student knows which type they will fly and which coast they will go to. Either the west coast at Camp Pendleton, or the east coast at Marine Corps Air Station New River, North Carolina.

"It's a competition, so the better you do, the more likely you are to get exactly what you want. If you're placed further down the list, you get what's left. They try to manage what we call the quality spread, ensuring that on the average, the outstanding performers are getting spread across all three Marine Aircraft Wings, a process that is also used for the other performers."

MARINE LIGHT ATTACK HELICOPTER TRAINING SQUADRON 303

Czech Air Force Training

Following the Czech Republic's 2019 selection of the H-1 to modernise its helicopter fleet with a mixed-fleet of four AH-1Z Vipers and eight UH-1Y Venoms, Czech aircrews trained with HMLAT-303 at Pendleton. Explaining, Lt Col Caster said: "The Czech students completed the exact same programme as US Marine Corps students: a 26-week programme for pilots and a 20-week programme for crew chiefs. Additionally, a group of Czech maintenance personnel spent time with 303."

As Bell gains foreign military sales, the company works with Naval Air Systems Command's Light/Attack Helicopter Programs Office, PMA-276 to set-up an initial training programme. The Slovak government is looking to procure the AH-1Z. Discussions about crew training are underway with PMA-276, with a view to Slovak personnel starting their introductory training with HMLAT-303. A Slovak delegation has visited HMLAT-303 for a site visit, but the process of establishing a syllabus, together with gaining funding and clearances takes time such that Lt Col Caster is unlikely to welcome any Slovak students in the time remaining as the squadron commanding officer.

"There are different requirements for introductory training based on platform requirements which differ between multi-piloted or crew aircraft and single seat aircraft. So, VMFAT-502 [the Miramar-based F-35B fleet replacement squadron] has different requirement for its introductory training than we do at HMLAT-303. So, foreign service training will be different for each platform. The training that 303 provides is foundational; learning how to fly the aircraft safely, learning how to employ the aircraft's systems in a basic manner, so that the student can apply that training to tactics at later stages of their career. When the Czech students returned home, they had foundational training, and were then able to develop their own tactics."

Left: **A crew chief with Marine Light Attack Helicopter Training Squadron 303 (HMLAT-303) signals to UH-1Y pilots during pre-flight checks.** US Marine Corps/LCpl Daniel Childs

Left: **A UH-1Y helicopter hover taxies from its parking spot for take-off from Camp Pendleton.** US Marine Corps/LCpl Daniel Childs

Below: **The pilot of an AH-1Z assigned to HMLAT-303 hover taxies along the flight line at Camp Pendleton.** US Marine Corps/Cpl Sarah Marshall

MARINE HEAVY HELICOPTER SQUADRON 461

AMERICAN KING

Marine Heavy Helicopter Squadron 461 (HMH-461) 'Ironhorse' based at MCAS New River in North Carolina is the first unit to operate the brand-new CH-53K King Stallion.

THE SIKORSKY CH-53K King Stallion is currently in US Marine Corps service with HMH-461 and Marine Test and Evaluation Squadron 1 (VMX-1), and with Naval Air Systems Command's Air Test and Evaluation Squadron Two One (HX-21). The CH-53K programme is managed by US Marine Corps Colonel Kate Fleeger who runs the H-53 Heavy Lift Helicopters Program Office PMA-261.

Discussing various current aspects of the CH-53K programme, Col Fleeger said: "We delivered the 15th CH-53K aircraft to HMH-461 on July 24 followed by another two in 2024, and six next year. We have 71 on contract for the US Marine Corps, either delivered or to be delivered, and 12 on contract with Sikorsky for Israel which has an option for another six. Additionally, Japan and the Republic of South Korea are interested in procuring the CH-53K: up to 18 for Korea and around five for Japan. We've got a few other countries on the radar as well.

"In November 2022 we passed our full-rate production milestone which gave us the authority to move forward with production lots. Now we have the first two full-rate production lots under contract. In FY2025 we plan to award the next lots and are considering a two-year block buy or potentially a five-year, multi-year buy. From a contracting perspective, we are on schedule with putting the individual lots on contract from a programmatic plan perspective.

"The CH-53K has completed developmental test and is now into follow on test and evaluation [FOT&E] with VMX-1 at Yuma and HX-21 here at Pax. FOT&E will be recurring. Last September, we flew our last developmental test flight, and the four aircraft used [partly owned by Sikorsky] are now fully owned by the United States government and remain here at Pax. But we still have some developmental ground tests to complete, some analysis and report writing through 2025.

"When the US Marine Corps declared the CH-53K with initial operating capability in April 2022, one of the items that they assessed was the support equipment, both common support equipment and peculiar support equipment. As the fleet

Below: A CH-53K King Stallion lifts F-35C Lightning II test aircraft CF-01 while being aerial refuelled by a KC-130T tanker on the 305nm flight between NAS Patuxent River and Lakehurst, New Jersey, on April 24, 2024.
Naval Air Systems Command/Kyra Helwick

MARINE HEAVY HELICOPTER SQUADRON 461

Right: US Marines with 3rd Battalion, 4th Marine Regiment, 1st Marine Division, board a Sikorsky CH-53K King Stallion during an air transport training event at Marine Corps Air Ground Combat Center, Twentynine Palms, California.
US Marine Corps/ LCpl Colton Brownlee

US NAVY AND MARINE CORPS YEARBOOK **2024**

MARINE HEAVY HELICOPTER SQUADRON 461

Above: US Marines with Combat Logistics Battalion 26 prepare for an external heavy lift by a CH-53K King Stallion assigned to Marine Heavy Helicopter Squadron 461 (HMH-461), as part of Weapons and Tactics Instructor 1-24 near Yuma, Arizona, on October 10, 2023. US Marine Corps/Cpl Rowdy Vanskike

continues to fly and maintain the aircraft, the efficacy of the support equipment is continually assessed to make sure we don't need to make improvements or produce additional equipment that would benefit the Marines and how they maintain the aircraft. We already have projects underway for additional support equipment.

"The CH-53K is the most data rich aircraft that we currently have in the Department of Navy. The data gets fed into a central location, so the programme office has access to it, and we're monitoring for trends over time. That's been one of our success stories, not only from an identification of potential issues, but also from identification of components that we can keep on wing longer, thereby reducing the amount of maintenance required on the fleet squadron, and reducing overall cost, because we are only replacing components when they need to be replaced, and not at set number of hours."

Discussing the most recent notable event to involve a CH-53K, Col Fleeger said: "On April 24, a CH-53K flown by a crew assigned to VMX-1 lifted an F-35C test aircraft from Naval Air Station Patuxent River to the prototype, manufacturing and test department of the Naval Air Warfare Center Aircraft Division at Lakehurst, New Jersey for use in future emergency recovery systems testing. One photo shows the CH-53K carrying another aircraft [the F-35C] while aerial refuelling behind a KC-130T, which shows one example of how the CH-53K will integrate into the Marine Air-Ground Task Force operational construct utilising its extended range through aerial refuelling, and its heavy external lift capability."

A NAVAIR press release gave details of the mission: "Minutes after 11.00AM, the almost 100-foot-long helicopter lifted the approximately 22,000-pound airframe from Patuxent River and headed out over the Chesapeake to begin the 305 nautical mile transport. The CH-53K is currently cleared to lift loads up to 36,000lb."

Col Fleeger also discussed a nascent milestone: "In the next couple of years will be the first deployment. The programme office is closely tracking that work-up to make sure that everyone across the enterprise is ready to support the aircraft when it goes on its first deployment. We want to make sure that once we start deploying the CH-53K out of the east coast, we can continue to do so."

Ironhorse and the King

Discussing CH-53K fleet operations with pilots serving with HMH-461, the squadron's executive officer, Major Joseph

Hawkinson said: "We currently operate 11 CH-53K aircraft and are working toward full operational capability declaration. At least twice a year we fly in support of the weapons and tactics instructor course at Yuma and complete various training detachments throughout the country, as we continue to build for future deployments. Each WTI had its own significant milestones.

"Our first WTI in March 2023 was focused on integrating the new CH-53K aircraft with other marine corps assets involved and showcased the helicopter's capabilities, most notably, on March 28, by lifting a 36,000lb load, which remains the heaviest load that a US Department of Defense aircraft has lifted outside of developmental test.

"In June 2023 we conducted a tail-to-tail transfer of a standard 463L pallet from a KC-130J to one of our aircraft which is a large increase in capability over the CH-53E, the E-model's cabin space was not large enough to accommodate a 463L pallet. This capability allows a CH-53K to haul cargo from a C-17 or a C-130 on a remote runway, and in a short period of time, load a 463L pallet onto a CH-53K for distribution throughout the battlefield. The event took place at MCAS New River working with a KC-130J assigned to Marine Aerial Refueler Transport Squadron 252 (VMGR-252). The KC-130J pilot landed the aircraft and positioned the aircraft tail-to-tail with our CH-53K. Marines quickly moved the cargo from aboard the KC-130J into our CH-53K cargo cabin as a static proof of concept. The capability reduces the time required to transfer cargo from a fixed wing aircraft to the battlefield.

"On October 20, 2023, we were tasked by the Naval Safety Center to assist them with the recovery of an MH-60S Seahawk that went down in the Inyo National Forest near Mammoth Lakes, California. The crash site was over 9,000ft above mean sea level. We were asked to participate while we were conducting training for WTI because the CH-53K is the only asset within the US DoD with sufficient power to lift another aircraft at that altitude. We sent two aircraft, a primary and an alternate, successfully recovered the MH-60S and safely transferred it back to its home station. The immediate terrain around the crash site was narrow which presented the crew with very marginal clearances between the rotor blades and obstacles located around the crash site. The lift was made more challenging due to the altitude and high winds."

Cargo Delivery and Free Fall

HMH-461's operations officer, Major Lee Henderson served with VMX-1 when the test squadron conducted day and night aerial cargo delivery and military freefall operations with a CH-53K. Explaining the evaluations, Major Henderson said: "For the cargo air delivery, we loaded four pallets in the aircraft. We were operating from an outlying field called Oak Grove north of New River. We flew a rosette pattern over the field at different altitudes to drop pallets to verify metrics. For example, offset to use based on the winds. We completed test during the daytime and at night. For the free fall, we climbed to 10,000 feet from where the Marines qualified in parachuting jumped out of the back of the aircraft to verify the procedures used with the CH-53E are safe for the CH-53K. The tests were all completed by VMX-1's CH-53K then based at Marine Corps Station New River."

Maj Henderson also detailed another notable tasking: "In March 2024, HMH-461 assisted with the 22nd Marine Expeditionary Unit's offload, which involved carrying cargo in the cargo compartment from the San Antonio-class amphibious transport dock ship USS *Kearsarge* [LHD-3] to shore."

First Deployment: The Early Preparations

Discussing HMH-461's ongoing preparations for the CH-53K's first deployment with a Marine Expeditionary Unit (MEU), Major Hawkinson said: "Over the course of the last couple of years, we've been able to build a cadre of CH-53K pilots that are now qualifying as aircraft commanders and section leads and will be qualified to deploy with the MEU by the end of FY2025 and then deploy in FY2026. HMH-461 is also the CH-53K model manager, so we are employed as a an operational squadron, but we also oversee the evaluation and improvement of the aircraft's publications, and act as the primary training squadron, providing instruction for new pilots who are beginning their training on the CH-53K or who are transitioning from a different platform. We are building up a core cadre

Below: **US Marines with Marine Heavy Helicopter Squadron 461 (HMH-461) and 2nd Distribution Support Battalion execute the lift of a downed US Navy MH-60S Seahawk at Inyo National Forest, California, on October 20, 2023.** US Marine Corps/Cpl Rowdy Vanskike

MARINE HEAVY HELICOPTER SQUADRON 461

The combined efforts of marines, sailors, and Forest Service personnel allowed HMH-461 to successfully recover an MH-60S Seahawk with a CH-53K King Stallion at Inyo National Forest, California, on October 20, 2023. US Marine Corps/Cpl Rowdy Vanskike

that will move to the CH-53 training squadron, HMHT-302 [Marine Heavy Helicopter Training Squadron 302 based at New River], which will train, educate, and mentor squadrons through their transition from CH-53E to CH-53K."

The CH-53K's primary mission set is to transport Marines, heavy equipment and supplies during ship-to-shore movement in support of amphibious assault and subsequent operations ashore. Discussing this role, Major Hawkinson said: "Our primary integration with marine ground units has been the WTI support in Yuma, which included combat assault transport of Marine forces, aerial delivery of heavy equipment and logistical supplies, and tactical recovery of personnel. During

these integration events, we focused on platform familiarisation, planning, briefing, and executing with marine ground forces. Additionally, we have supported Marine Forces Special Operations Command [MARSOC] in various events to facilitate their training and readiness, as well as our own. We completed a 2nd Marine Aircraft Wing distributed aviation operations exercise moving Marines, cargo and fuel between Florida and the Bahamas island chain."

Concluding, Maj Hawkinson said: "Our Marines are focused daily on training and employing the CH-53K to ensure we have capable combat crews ready to go when the nation calls."

MARINE FIGHTER ATTACK TRAINING SQUADRON 502

F-35B PILOT TRAINING

Marine Fighter Attack Training Squadron 502 (VMFAT-502) is the US Marine Corps' west coast F-35B fleet replacement squadron. **Mark Ayton** spoke with the squadron executive officer, Lieutenant Colonel Sean Callison, about its operations.

THE PRIMARY MISSION for VMFAT-502 is to train student pilots following their graduation from flight school with about 200 to 300 hours to their name. They will usually previously have flown the T-6 Texan for their primary flight training and then the T-45 Goshawk for their intermediate and advanced flight training stage. On graduation a student gets their wings and moves to a fleet replacement squadron. If the student is selected for the F-35B, they will go to either VMFAT-501 based at MCAS Beaufort, South Carolina or VMFAT-502 based at MCAS Miramar, California.

Lieutenant Colonel Sean Callison serves as the executive officer of VMFAT-502. As a Harrier pilot, he went through the F-35B course with VMFAT-501 at Beaufort and then served as an instructor on 501. During his time as an IP with 501, VMFAT-502 stood-up at MCAS Beaufort, South Carolina and subsequently moved to MCAS Miramar, California. Lt Col Callison was asked if he wanted to move to Miramar. An easy decision since San Diego is his hometown. He arrived at Miramar in May, 2022.

Lt Col Callison is a qualified US Marine Corps weapons and tactics instructor, one of five assigned to VMFAT-502. Three completed the WTI course either in the Hornet or the Harrier, and two completed the course in the F-35B..

F-35B Course

Explaining the F-35B course, Lt Col Callison said: "We provide the baseline

Below: **This VMFAT-502 F-35B is fitted with a GAU-22 external gun pod.** US Marine Corps/Sgt Sean Potter

US NAVY AND MARINE CORPS YEARBOOK **2024**

MARINE FIGHTER ATTACK TRAINING SQUADRON 502

Right: **An F-35B Lightning II assigned to Marine Fighter Attack Training Squadron 502 (VMFAT-502) during an aerial refuelling training mission over Southern California. VMFAT-502 and KC-130J-equipped Marine Aerial Refueler Transport Squadron 352 (VMGR-352) conducted training that enabled F-35B student pilots to achieve proficiency in aerial refuelling operations.** US Marine Corps/Sgt Sean Potter

for the tactics they will use in the future. We teach them how to safely fly the aircraft, but we rapidly move into teaching them fifth-generation tactics, which is a fundamental mindset shift from the fourth-generation tactics used by F-15, F-16, F/A-18, and Typhoon, which do not have fifth-generation capabilities inherent in stealth.

"Students have about a month to settle in before they start the syllabus which lasts for about 52 weeks, depending on how our throughput is with aircraft and pilot availability.

"We break the syllabus up into two phases, the mechanics phase, and the mission phase. Each phase is divided into stages. Students will progress through a single stage and then move

FIRST FLIGHT

Discussing the preparations undertaken for a student's first flight, Lt Col Callison said: "Students go through a robust emergency simulator syllabus, so they are ready once they get in the aircraft. The sims deal with complex emergencies that could happen, though the likelihood is very low. I've got nearly 600 hours in the F-35B, and I've had to return to the airfield, maybe three or four times due to emergency.

"We also put them through what we call a taxi exam when they strap into the aircraft, do everything as if they were going to fly, taxi out to the runway, but don't take-off. This helps alleviate some of the jitters, and some of the consternation with getting into the aircraft, things that they don't get in the sim, how the aircraft shakes and how it feels when you taxi.

"We chase the student flying the F-35B for the first time in another aircraft and have someone in a truck out on the airfield watching to make sure the landing gear is down, that they're not landing on the wrong runway, that they're not landing without clearance, all as a safety backstop.

"First flight is stressful, so the more things we can do to eliminate the jitters until take-off, the better. I had 1,000 hours in the Harrier, and I was like, this is stupid. I know how to taxi, but to be perfectly honest the taxi exam was probably one of the best events in the syllabus.

US NAVY AND MARINE CORPS YEARBOOK **2024**

MARINE FIGHTER ATTACK TRAINING SQUADRON 502

on to the next stage. The syllabus is, for the most part, regimented, but there are some deviations allowed in situations when we can take one stage and put it in front of the other.

"The mechanics phase starts with the familiarisation stage when they learn how to fly the aircraft, fly the landing pattern, fly using instruments, and teach them how to fly the F-35B in STOVL, the short take-off, vertical landing mode, both in the take-off and landing environments.

"During the familiarisation stage, students do an abundance of sims to get them ready to fly the aircraft. Because there's no two-seat variant, the first time they fly the F-35B is by themselves.

"They do a series of sims working the STOVL landing pattern here at the field followed by two flights that are dedicated strictly to STOVL operations, where they practice landing on the runway via what we call slow landings. When we land conventionally, we fly the approach at about 150-160kts. In STOVL we're landing to the runway at about 100kts, but we can land as slow as 50kts to the runway.

"The next flight is dedicated solely to landing vertically involving multiple vertical landings. The aircraft is configured with a lower fuel weight to maintain the performance to land. They'll do a couple of landings, they'll get them a squirt of gas, and go do it again until they get it right. They'll do that day and night.

"Then they move into basic tactics, where they start working on the principles of air-to-air employment during two flights. This is followed by either air-to-surface or basic fighter manoeuvres, to learn how to employ the jet, utilising the aircraft's sensors to find surface targets and employ the ordnance to destroy surface targets.

"Basic fighter manoeuvres or BFM, is a standard dog fighting syllabus involving offensive, defensive, and what we call high aspect when you start the fight at a neutral position. The first couple of flights will be offensive, then they progress into defensive, and then they go into the high aspect with a neutral start to the fight, followed by trying to apply the principles they have already learned to gain a tactical advantage.

"They then move on to tactical intercepts, which takes the concept of air-to-air employment and introduces the student to how we employ as a section, a flight of two, or a division, as a flight of four. Flying as a division requires a team mindset. How we employ as a team, and how we fight the aircraft as a flight of two or flight of four.

"The final element of the mechanics phase is called tactical intercepts, students then go into the mission phase, where they will do close air support, armed reconnaissance, and anti-air warfare where they work on protecting a simulated ship or a simulated airfield. They also do offensive counter air, when they push forward into enemy territory, and look to eliminate [the] enemy air picture out there. We also do suppression of enemy air defence as part of the mechanics' phase."

The syllabus culminates with the strike flight, in which students fly against Red Air and simulated surface-to-air missile systems while trying to ingress a target area and employ ordnance.

A night syllabus introduces the student to night-time flying and incorporates some of the mission sets already conducted at night.

Explaining other aspects of 502's course, Lt Col Callison said: "We do not incorporate any sorties that involve working cooperatively with other marine corps assets, but students do get a small introduction to that in the

Above: **Joins and seals can be seen in the bright Californian sunshine atop an F-35B assigned to VMFAT-502.**
US Marine Corps/ Sgt Sean Potter

Right: **An F-35B assigned to VMFAT-502 plugged into the drogue trailed on the hose from a KC-130J.**
US Marine Corps/ Sgt Sean Potter

HARRIER OR F-35B?

Comparing the F-35B with the AV-8B Harrier, Lt Col Callison said: "The F-35B is a lot easier to fly than the Harrier because I'm not trying to fight while flying the aircraft as per the Harrier. I like how much situational awareness I have in the aircraft. I know what's around me and what's going on around me, which helps with tactically employing the aircraft. The F-35B is computer driven, going into a hover I press two buttons, and the jet will hover on its own. It's very easy to hover. The Harrier is much more fun to fly because there are no computers to help you out."

MARINE FIGHTER ATTACK TRAINING SQUADRON 502

sim. It's an in-house course, where it's F-35 pretty much all the way through. It's set-up that way to bring students up to speed before they get assigned to a fleet squadron."

F-35 Syllabus

"The entirety of the F-35 syllabus is broken down into levels, so 1000 level, 2000 level, 3000 level, 4000 level. VMFAT-502's course is 1000 level only."

Level 1000, Core Skill Introduction
Entry level training required to receive or be eligible for assignment of a primary MOS. Includes such training as systems/equipment, operations familiarisation, initial crew procedures, and initial exposure to core skills.

Level 2000, Core Skills
Fundamental, environmental, or conditional capabilities required to perform basic functions. These basic functions serve as tactical enablers that allow crews to progress to the more complex mission skills.

Level 3000, Mission Skills
Mission skills enable a unit to execute a specific mission essential task (MET). They are comprised of advanced event(s) that are focused on MET performance and draw upon the knowledge, abilities, and situational awareness developed during core skill training.

MARINE FIGHTER ATTACK TRAINING SQUADRON 502

Level 4000, Core Plus Skill
Training events that can be theatre specific or that have a low likelihood of occurrence. They may be fundamental, environmental, or conditional capabilities required to perform basic functions.

Discussing Level 4000 training, Lt Col Callison said: "Integration with MEU or MAGTF type assets is 4000 level which a student is probably not going to encounter until they do some sort of service level exercise, or they're in a pre-deployment training programme, i.e. when they're getting attached to a MEU."

Below: US Marine Corps/Sgt Sean Potter

MARINE FIGHTER ATTACK TRAINING SQUADRON 502

Training Events

Explaining 502's current declared status, Lt Col Callison said: "We opened the doors of VMFAT-502 at MCAS Beaufort, South Carolina in June 2020 when the squadron was focused on getting the instructor pilot, cadre, ready to go. The squadron moved to MCAS Miramar, California in January 2022 and subsequently started training students, the numbers for which have steadily increased each year. Today 502 is almost at full rate production capacity, with regards to students, and should achieve full rate production capacity next year."

MARINE FIGHTER ATTACK TRAINING SQUADRON 502

VMFAT-502 is the second US Marine Corps F-35B fleet replacement squadron, the first is VMFAT-501. Both squadrons are concurrently training new F-35B pilots, as Lt Col Callison explained: "Currently, 501 has a greater pilot training requirement than 502 purely because of our ongoing journey to FOC status. In the next year or two, we will nearly equal 501's annual output."

When student pilots graduate from their course with 502, they can be posted to any F-35B squadron regardless of its location. Detailing the process, Lt Col Callison said: "Once students are about halfway through the syllabus, we will talk to the officers in charge of issuing them orders to the squadron the Marine Corps needs to fill. They will go to any of the four locations that operates F-35Bs: Iwakuni, Japan, Yuma, Arizona, Beaufort, South Carolina, or Cherry Point, North Carolina. VMFA-533 is currently standing at Beaufort alongside 501."

In March 2023, VMFAT-502 undertook a deployment for training or DFT to Naval Air Station New Orleans, Louisiana. In January, 2024, 502 completed a DFT to Naval Air Station Jacksonville, Florida.

Explaining the objectives of a DFT, Lt Col Callison said: "From a training aspect, a DFT allows our students, our maintainers, and our instructors to operate from a different base in a different area. From a marine corps perspective, it allows us to gain experience of operating outside of our comfort zone. We're operating from an unfamiliar airfield, with unfamiliar ranges, and unfamiliar maintenance operations. It allows us to pick up the squadron, move it somewhere, get set up and operate.

"DFT flight operations add in some additional stress regarding the administrative portion of the flight because it's an unfamiliar airfield. They've got to get familiar with what's around

MARINE FIGHTER ATTACK TRAINING SQUADRON 502

Left: **F-35B BuNo 169414/WF559 assigned to VMFAT-502 seen landing at Naval Air Facility El Centro, California.**
Chris Wood

Below: **F-35B BuNo 169413/WF558 seen on take-off from Naval Air Facility El Centro, California.**
Chris Wood

them, how far away the range is, how much gas they will need to get back? These are important things for students to consider when they are preparing for a flight. Ultimately, they will be flying as a wingman, so the flight lead has the burden of that, but we still want them to prepare and understand the information provided.

"We are striving to do two DFTs a year with the intent of going to locations with better training aids. We already deploy to Mountain Home Air Force Base, Idaho which has a range equipped with robust surface-to-air threat emitters, which helps to improve our training a lot."

Course Evolution

Since Lt Col Callison started flying the F-35B in 2020, the evolution of the aircraft's mission systems and the capabilities have increased with software upgrades and hardware modifications. Consequently, the ability

MARINE FIGHTER ATTACK TRAINING SQUADRON 502

Above: **The pilot of VMFAT-502 F-35B BuNo 169295/WF552 retracts the landing gears during while overshooting Naval Air Facility El Centro, California.**
Chris Wood

for the aircraft to do more advanced things has also increased, which poses the question to instructor pilots and students alike, what can the F-35 do? Explaining, Lt Col Callison said: "We want our students to understand the latest pacing threats because those are the threats we train to. As our adversaries are advancing, we are updating how we employ the aircraft based on those threats. In reference to area of employment, our tactics behind area employment have probably changed five times in the past four years, so it continues to evolve."

Applicability to the F-35B

Discussing student aptitude for absorbing information generated by the aircraft, Lt Col Callison made the comparison with when he went the through the Harrier course with VMAT-203 at Cherry Point: "Our baseline threat was an SA-6, now the baseline is an SA-6 extending through to employing against an integrated air defence system [IADS]. Our students have a very good understanding of what an IADS looks like from that perspective, and they pick up on the digitisation of the jet very quickly. For the most part, there are very few issues with students picking up on the digitisation. They're able to take in a lot of information and process it rapidly. This jet generates a lot of information, so it's crucial that the student can interpret that information at the right time and be able to act on that information.

MARINE FIGHTER ATTACK TRAINING SQUADRON 502

"Students will make errors. But when you show them in the debrief and say, hey, you need to be doing this, and then give them what we call the instructional fix on the backside of that, they usually, for the most part, get that information, and after they've made that error, they're probably not going to make that error again. Sometimes it takes more than one or two iterations, but for the most part, they can fix their error by taking the information given by the instructor and apply it to their next sim flight.

"Students must pass every event. If they do not meet the standard for an event, we'll grade them with an unsatisfactory flight, and then the instructor cadre analyse why the student got an unsatisfactory event. Then we'll investigate the event and notice, for example, that the student landed on the wrong runway. Okay, that was a momentary lapse in situational awareness. Then we ask ourselves whether we really need them to fly an entire sortie again?

"In other instances when the student is not meeting the performance standard, we advise them that they're either not getting the sight picture or they're not doing something right and need to fix the problem by giving them extra instruction. We usually give them a couple of extra training events and then they re-fly the event. For the most part that's enough to get them over the line."

FIFTH-GENERATION TIGERS

Marine Fighter Attack Squadron 542 (VMFA-542) 'Tigers' is the first east coast, frontline, F-35B squadron to stand-up in the 2nd Marine Aircraft Wing.

THE FIRST MARINES posted to 542 from training arrived at Marine Corps Air Station Cherry Point, North Carolina in October 2022. At that point, some Marines assigned to VMA-542, the Harrier squadron, were deployed with a Marine Expeditionary Unit (MEU) operating under a VMM. They returned to Cherry Point in November.

The Harrier-equipped VMA-542 officially sunset on December 1, 2022. At the time, the squadron's new F-35 hangar was not complete leaving the squadron 'homeless' until January 2023, when the new shelter was ready. In February 2023, a large contingent of 542's maintenance personnel who were unfamiliar with the F-35B went to Marine Fighter Attack Training Squadron 501 (VMFAT-501) at Marine Corps Air Station Beaufort in South Carolina for six weeks of hands-on training to familiarise themselves with the F-35B prior to 542 receiving its first aircraft.

Explaining, Lieutenant Colonel Brian Hansell, the commanding officer of the squadron since the start of its F-35B transition said: "Our manning throughout that time continued to grow so we were able to start standing up the necessary programmes, maintenance for example. We maintained our close relationship with VMFAT-501 which deployed to Cherry Point for short periods of time to fly their aircraft from our flight lines to enable our Marines to get comfortable with using our flight lines and to keep them proficient and current on the F-35B.

"Our first aircraft was delivered direct from the Lockheed Martin Fort Worth factory toward the end of May. From that point in time, our maintainers were maintaining our own aircraft, but we were not yet declared as safe for flight. That's the designation awarded to a squadron once the required safety, maintenance, and operational inspections are passed. Back then we were flying under the authority and cognizance of VMFAT-501's commander at Beaufort. On August 11, 2023, the squadron was certified as safe for flight with three aircraft on our books. We held a squadron redesignation ceremony, formally becoming Marine Fighter Attack Squadron 542 [VMFA-542]. My title changed from officer in charge to commanding officer."

First Detachment: Florida's Emerald Coast

"In September, we made our first detachment. Our destination was Tyndall Air Force Base, Florida to execute a weapons system evaluation programme

Left: An F-35B with VMFA-542 taxies down the runway at Tyndall Air Force Base, Florida, during a Weapons System Evaluation Program. US Marine Corps/Cpl Christopher Hernandez

Below: Marines with VMFA-542 perform pre-flight inspections on an F-35B at Tyndall Air Force Base, Florida. The Naval Weapons System Evaluation Program allowed VMFA-542 to safely conduct the loading and firing of live missiles at threat-realistic targets to test the squadron's ability, flexibility, and procedures while repositioned in unfamiliar locations. US Marine Corps/Cpl Christopher Hernandez

MARINE FIGHTER ATTACK SQUADRON 542

[WSEP] during which we received training for shooting air-to-air missiles and launched seven missiles. We targeted a WSEP at Tyndall for our first squadron detachment because the conditions were appropriate for a young squadron: three weeks long, not too difficult a movement, and plenty of support available from the respective F-35-equipped wings at both Tyndall and Eglin Air Force Base.

"We also wanted to practice a movement shortly after our safe for flight declaration in preparation for a scheduled deployment to Norway in February 2024. The deployment to Tyndall proved beneficial; the squadron got good training, our ordnance Marines got to load missiles, some of our pilots got to shoot missiles, and our maintenance Marines generated the aircraft."

According to Air Combat Command: "The 53d Weapons Evaluation Group [53rd WEG] is an Air Combat Command tenant organization that reports to the 53d Wing located at Eglin Air Force Base, Florida.

"The 53rd WEG comprises five squadrons and two detachments at four geographically separated locations, of which the 53d Test Support Squadron, 81st Air Control Squadron, 82nd Aerial Targets Squadron, and the 83rd Fighter Weapons Squadron are all located at Tyndall.

"The 53rd WEG conducts the US Air Force air-to-air and air-to-ground Weapons System Evaluation Programs, known as WSEP East (Tyndall AFB) and WSEP West (Hill AFB), under Combat Air Forces (CAF) Plan 53, among others.

"Unit personnel provide all USAF aerial target support for Department of Defense (DoD) and international partners in the Eglin-Gulf ranges. The WSEP team includes US Navy F/A-18 and F-35 subject matter experts who work alongside their USAF colleagues.

Right: **Marines with VMFA-542 perform maintenance on an F-35B at Tyndall Air Force Base, Florida.**
US Marine Corps/ Cpl Christopher Hernandez

Below: **Marines with VMFA-542 pose for a photo at Tyndall Air Force Base, Florida.**
US Marine Corps/ Cpl Christopher Hernandez

"Annually, WSEP reports and identifies weapons system performance and deficiencies, including recommendations for corrective action directly to the United States Air Force Warfare Center, Air Combat Command, and the Chief of Staff of the Air Force."

Clarifying, Lt Col Hansell said: "VMFA-542's participation in a WSEP was not a formal requirement on our road to IOC and when we discussed the possibility with my leadership, they gave their full support. Despite the inclusion of a WSEP on 542's journey to IOC, other VMFA F-35 squadrons reached IOC without completing a WSEP. I think it's an intelligent thing to do, as you look to build and gain experience in your squadron."

Initial Operating Capability

The squadron's next big milestone was achieving initial operating capability (IOC). Explaining, Lt Col Hansell said: "For that, you need a certain number of aircraft, you need to have a certain number of aircrews trained in our mission essential tasks, you need a certain readiness number, and you need a certain number of people in your squadron, so it's all our reporting metrics.

"At that point, from a pilot training perspective we had enough aircraft to start making progress. Most of our training involves flying as part of a four-ship, so you need at least six aircraft to be able to do that. So, we mapped out all training events that we were required to execute to declare IOC and started working hard to accomplish that. We tried to project a deliberate path to get our IOC declaration and followed that path. We didn't race to it but tried to get there as intelligently as possible. We've had high readiness throughout the period with very consistent ops from Cherry Point.

"Marine Corps squadrons frequently go on cross country trips at weekends, and we flew a lot of cross-country flights. For young air crew, it's a great experience, to go to an unfamiliar field and learn the ins and outs of operating from the airfield, and for getting training at different locations. Though most of our training occurred at Cherry Point, we averaged about two weekends a month flying cross-country flights.

"Typically, squadron maintainers go with the cross-country flights, not because they're required, but because they're desired to enable smoother operations. At some of the airfields we went to, the airfield personnel weren't willing to fuel our aircraft, so we would utilise either the maintainers or the pilots to fuel our aircraft themselves.

"Personnel other than Marines don't understand how to climb into and get out of the jet, or how to unstow a boarding ladder, so we prefer to send a small support team because it makes things go smoother."

VMFA-542 declared initial operational capability on February 5, 2024, just days before the squadron deployed to Norway. The squadron's tenth jet was delivered immediately after it returned to Cherry Point which meant the squadron was fully established and was able to declare full operational capability shortly afterwards.

Lt Col Hansell said: "The declaration meant that VMFA-542 had enough operational F-35B aircraft, trained pilots, maintainers, and support equipment to self-sustain its mission essential tasks, that is close-air support, offensive anti-air warfare, strike coordination and reconnaissance, suppression of enemy air defences, electronic attack, electronic support, and active air defence.

"VMFA-542 is the first operational fifth-generation squadron in II Marine Expeditionary Force, giving the aviation combat element the most lethal, survivable, and interoperable strike fighter in the US inventory. The F-35B is unmatched in its capability to support Marines against the advanced threats that we can expect in the future."

Exercise Nordic Response 2024

According to Lt Col Hansell, deploying to Norway was by far the heaviest lift for VMFA-542 thus far: "It required a tremendous amount of preparation work and planning, just because it was a large exercise, involving a large Marine component transiting over to Norway - multiple Marine Corps squadrons and ground personnel from both the 2nd Marine Aircraft Wing and II Marine Expeditionary Force."

Above: **Marines with VMFA-542 wait on the flight line at Tyndall Air Force Base, Florida.**
US Marine Corps/ Cpl Christopher Hernandez

Left: **A fixed-wing mechanic with VMFA-542 closes a panel on an F-35B at Tyndall Air Force Base, Florida during a Weapon System Evaluation Program.**
US Marine Corps/ Cpl Christopher Hernandez

MARINE FIGHTER ATTACK SQUADRON 542

Right: **Lieutenant Colonel Brian Hansell, Marine Fighter Attack Squadron 542 commanding officer, prepares for flight operations at Marine Corps Air Station Cherry Point, North Carolina.** US Marine Corps/ SSgt Daisha Ramirez

Right: **The WH tail code of an F-35B assigned to Marine Fighter Attack Squadron 542 (VMFA-542).** US Marine Corps/ Cpl Christopher Hernandez

Below: **An F-35B assigned to VMFA-542 taxies at Tyndall Air Force Base, Florida during a Weapon System Evaluation Program which allowed the squadron to safely conduct the loading and firing of live missiles at threat-realistic targets.** US Marine Corps/ Cpl Christopher Hernandez

Expeditionary Force, arrived in Norway between February 16-25, in preparation for Exercise Nordic Response 24.

"The 2nd MAW deployed F-35Bs assigned to Marine Fighter Attack Squadron 542 (VMFA-542), F/A-18 Hornets with VMFA-312, and KC-130J Super Hercules with Marine Aerial Refueler Transport Squadron 252 (VMGR-252). Both VMFA-542 and VMGR-252 deployed from their home base at Marine Corps Air Station Cherry Point, North Carolina, and VMFA-312 deployed from its home base of MCAS Beaufort, South Carolina."

Exercise Nordic Response 24 was VMFA-542's first overseas exercise as an F-35B Lightning II squadron and its first exercise since achieving IOC on February 5. IOC means that VMFA-542 has enough operational F-35B Lightning II aircraft, trained pilots, maintainers, and support equipment to self-sustain its mission essential tasks (METs).

During the exercise, VMFA-542 employed its F-35Bs in a near-peer adversary training exercise while advancing and sustaining the squadron in its core METs of anti-air warfare, active air defence, suppression-of-enemy air defence, and strike capabilities while progressing the squadron toward full operational capability. VMFA-542 integrated with aircraft operated by NATO allies from across northern Europe including F-35s from the Royal Norwegian Air Force and the RAF.

Other US Marine Corps squadrons involved included Marine Fighter Attack Squadron 312 (VMFA-312) which employed its F/A-18C and F/A-18D Hornets in combined military air operations to increase its cold-weather capabilities and proficiency, aircrew qualifications, and concepts of distributed operations.

According to II MEF: "Nordic Response was a Norwegian national readiness and defence exercise designed to enhance military capabilities and allied cooperation in a high-intensity arctic environment. The exercise tested military activities ranging from the reception of allied and partner reinforcements, command and control interoperability to combined joint operations, maritime prepositioning for logistics, integration with NATO militaries, and reacting against an adversary force during a dynamic training environment.

"US Marine Corps aircraft and personnel from three flying squadrons with the 2nd Marine Aircraft Wing [MAW] and II Marine

MARINE FIGHTER ATTACK SQUADRON 542

Marine Aerial Refueler Transport Squadron 253 (VMGR-252) employed its KC-130J aircraft to support the objectives of the Marine Air-Ground Task Force by providing cargo transportation, combat-assault transport, aerial refuelling, and aviation-delivered ground refuelling. VMGR-252 operated from expeditionary shore-based locations in cold-weather conditions.

Discussing VMFA-542's involvement, Lt Col Hansell said: "There was a large planning component for VMFA-542, making sure it was effective for all parties and in mission execution. The maintenance team had to move personnel and equipment across the Atlantic, a little different than just going to Florida. Ultimately, the logistics team was able to plan the movement for us and make sure it went smoothly.

"Any transatlantic movement of aircraft has the possibility of things not going according to plan, so we focused on the pilot training perspective to make sure that went smoothly. We flew the first leg between Beaufort and Keflavik, Iceland, stayed there overnight and then flew the final leg to Evenes, Norway, which is inside the Arctic Circle. That required us to aerial refuel from a strategic tanker, a so-called big wing tanker, so each pilot must

Above: An F-35B assigned to VMFA-542 taxies in front of two AV-8B Harrier II jets at Marine Corps Air Station Cherry Point, North Carolina.
US Marine Corps/Warrant Officer Akeel Austin

Right: F-35Bs with VMFA-542 prepare to taxi at Marine Corps Air Station Cherry Point, North Carolina.
US Marine Corps/LCpl Madison Blackstock

Below: US Marine Corps/Cpl Christopher Hernandez

get certified for strategic tanker aerial refuelling. Luckily, as part of the squadron's training build-up, we made sure all our pilots had recently aerial refuelled on a strategic tanker beforehand.

"Notable aspects of operations from Evenes from a maintenance perspective were operating from a Cold War airfield and parking our aircraft in hardened aircraft shelters. After returning from a mission, we taxied to the assigned shelter, made a 180° turn in a confined space, maintainers hooked the aircraft up to a winch, and then pulled them into the shelter which is a mountainside. An advanced party of maintenance personnel

got familiar with the winch system, elements of which had not been used for a long time, so there was a lot of working hand in hand with the Norwegians to get the winch systems working and making sure everything was safe to avoid any mishap.

"Because we wanted all nine of our aircraft deployed to Evenes and we didn't have any back-up aircraft, kudos to our maintenance team which did a great job in preparing all nine aircraft ready for the deployment, all of which successfully arrived as planned at Evenes. It was the first time the Marine Corps had deployed F-35s to the high north inside the Arctic

MARINE FIGHTER ATTACK SQUADRON 542

Circle and a lot of lessons were learned. The hardened shelters helped keep the temperature consistent, which helped aircraft readiness and reliability, which performed well out there.

"We flew with a lot of other countries, UK F-35Bs operating off HMS *Prince of Wales* and Norwegian F-35s. The Norwegians detached aircraft from Orland to Evenes and parked their aircraft alongside us. It was the first time a US Department of Defense squadron had operated from Evenes since the mid-1990s.

"We sent F-35s to Sweden, six days after it joined NATO on March 13, 2024, and undertook a distributed air operation exercise at Kallax airfield in the far north. It was the first time a US F-35 aircraft had landed in Sweden, the first time any F-35 had operated at Kallax, and one of the first training events conducted by Sweden as a NATO member. We also demonstrated to the Swedish Air Force how we conduct FARP operations, and how quickly we can refuel our aircraft, which involved cross training between the two services."

Marines assigned to Marine Aerial Refueler Transport Squadron 252 (VMGR-252) refuelled VMFA-542 F-35B aircraft at Kallax using aviation-delivered ground refuelling during a distributed aviation operation to showcase expeditionary advanced-base operations using host-nation support.

Lt Col Hansell said: "The whole point of the exercise was to generate a consistent battle rhythm of large force events involving 40-plus aircraft. We demonstrated geographically dispersed mission planning from five-plus sites including with the Brits onboard HMS *Prince of Wales* who mission planned from the boat. We were planning with whatever method was available, phones, email, and via secure internet. Aircraft participating in the exercise were dispersed and launched from those five-plus bases and met-up in the airspace, at the right time and at the right place to execute a mission.

"Nordic Response was hugely valuable. We returned from Norway fully up and running on the F-35B, operating at a high level. The deployment showcased unique aspects of the F-35 and its interoperability with the Brits, the Norwegians, the Swedes, and the Finns. It was great to be able to mission plan from geographically dispersed locations, for example, with Brits on a boat, the Norwegians at their part of the base, us at another part of the base, all following the same tactics, techniques, and procedures [TTPs]. To be able to speak a common language, to be able to launch and execute seamlessly, you wouldn't know if you had a British F-35 on your wing or if you had a Marine Corps F-35B on your wing, because they were truly interoperable.

"That's credit to the F-35 partnership and the fact that we all share common TTPs, common technology, digital interoperability, and the F-35 unique MADL data link seamlessly integrating between three different countries showed that every F-35 partner is a force multiplier. We got to test out the global spares pool. So, when we needed a part, frequently, that part would come from Orland, the main Royal Norwegian Air Force F-35 base, and experienced its value for when we take a Marine Corps F-35B squadron across the world, and plug right into the

Above: **Pilots with VMFA-542 stage in formation at Marine Corps Air Station Cherry Point, North Carolina.**
US Marine Corps/ LCpl Madison Blackstock

Below: **An F-35B assigned to VMFA-542 prepares to taxi at Marine Corps Air Station Cherry Point, North Carolina.**
US Marine Corps/ Cpl Adam Henke

MARINE FIGHTER ATTACK SQUADRON 542

global spares pool, and get parts from a fellow partner.

"It was great to fly with Finnish F/A-18s which proved to be seamless. We knew what to expect because we're used to flying with US Navy and US Marine Corps F/A-18s. I'd never flown with Gripens, and it was interesting to see the pros and cons of the aircraft and how the Swedes employ it. We're certainly focused on China, and we'll certainly deploy to that AOR based on the threat there. But the pleasure of being based on the east coast is the NATO AOR and we're focused on integrating with all the NATO countries."

Full Operational Capability

Achieving its IOC declaration meant that VMFA-542 was one step closer to achieving full operational capability (FOC). The squadron achieved FOC on April 3, which meant that VMFA-542 was ready to undertake full operations and had completed its transition from the legacy AV-8B Harrier to the F-35B Lightning II. FOC declaration meant VMFA-542 was capable and eligible to deploy globally in support of planned or contingency operations.

Commenting on the FOC declaration, Lt Col Hansell said: "This milestone marks the addition of a battle-ready aviation squadron with unmatched combat lethality and survivability to the Marine Expeditionary Force. We are ready and able to conduct missions globally in support of the MAGTF as we continue to prepare for the next challenge."

VMFA-542 began its transition to the F-35B Lightning II in December 2022 and received its first F-35B on May 31, 2023. The squadron then achieved IOC on February 5, before receiving its tenth aircraft on March 25, and achieved FOC on April 3.

Red Flag

The Nellis-based 414th Combat Training Squadron hosts Red Flag with a mission to maximise the combat readiness, capability, survivability, and interoperability of participating units. The squadron provides realistic, multi-domain training in a combined air, ground, space, and electronic threat environment while providing opportunities for a free exchange of ideas between forces.

Colonel Eric Winterbottom, 414th CTS commander said: "Training prioritises first timer's combat missions, mission commander upgrades, integration and flag unique experiences that contribute most to readiness and partnering.

"Aligning with the 2022 National Defense Strategy, Red Flag 24-3 focused on the Indo-Pacific Theatre

Above: **F-35B aircraft assigned to VMFA-542 lined-up on the flight line at Marine Corps Air Station Cherry Point, North Carolina prior to departure for Keflavik, Iceland.**
US Marine Corps/ Warrant Officer Akeel Austin

Below: **The nine F-35B aircraft assigned to VMFA-542 which deployed to Norway for Exercise Nordic Response 24 lined-up at Marine Corps Air Station Cherry Point, North Carolina prior to departure.**
US Marine Corps/ LCpl Madison Blackstock

and combating the pacing challenge. Red Flag is a large-scale exercise that aims to improve collaboration and interoperability among joint and interagency partners, contributing to the operational effectiveness of our nation's forces and those of our allies and partners."

The Red Flag commander said: "Participants engage with the 57th Wing's professional aggressors, integrate with coalition core function forces, and learn to keep faith with airmen through personnel recovery operations. This training is critical to enabling airmen to function independently making the mission more resilient and survivable. Participants will lead and learn in the world's best combat debrief, while writing the next chapter of the Red Flag's heritage."

Following Red Flag 24-3, which ran from July 22-August 2, 2024, squadrons forward deployed to a spoke location as part of an Air Force Warfare Center exercise called Bamboo Eagle which is designed to create a 'combat representative environment'

MARINE FIGHTER ATTACK SQUADRON 542

Right: **VMFA-542 F-35Bs taxi after a routine mission at Evenes Air Base, Norway during Exercise Nordic Response 24.**
US Marine Corps/LCpl Orlanys Diaz Figueroa

Right: US Marine Corps/Cpl Adam Henke

Below: US Marine Corps/LCpl Madison Blackstock

across large portions of the eastern Pacific Ocean.

Lieutenant Colonel Ian Osterreicher, USAF 34th Fighter Squadron commander, a participating unit in Red Flag 24-3 said: "Red Flag is scripted. The schedule is set. The different units get to talk face-to-face and mission plan together. Bamboo Eagle is not. There is no script. That's important because that's what will happen in conflict. You'll fly somewhere you've never been before, with people you've never worked with, and be asked to do something you've never done before."

Approximately 3,000 service members from four branches operated 150 aircraft from nearly a dozen locations to create the separate force elements of Bamboo Eagle. On a given day, the pilots flew a mission, met up with a tanker over the ocean, or completed a hot-pit refuel at another contingency location – then re-join the fight alongside US Air Force F-22s and F-35As, United States Marine Corps F-35Bs, or US Navy EA-18G Growlers. From a mission-planning perspective, the disaggregated

operations challenge the squadron to find solutions 'on the fly'.

Osterreicher said: "For 20 years in the Middle East we got used to doing the same mission over and over again from a set location. Now it's on us [the units] to provide our primary mission sets, dislocated, with little to no communication. Fly thousands of miles. Trust your tanker support is in the air for you to keep going. Talk to each other airborne and make it happen."

During Bamboo Eagle, F-35s were primarily tasked with offensive and defensive counter-air against fourth and fifth-generation aircraft, long range bombers and cruise missiles.

Osterreicher said: "Stealth, lethality, survivability. The F-35 excels at all those things. It provides the situational awareness pilots can lead with out there. Missions took place over the eastern Pacific Ocean in airspace that stretched west from the California coast, provided valuable opportunity to operate at ranges not normally available – testing the jet's capabilities as well as the pilot's mettle.

Above: **An F-35B assigned to VMFA-542 at Evenes Air Base, Norway during Exercise Nordic Response 24.**
US Marine Corps/ Warrant Officer Akeel Austin

"For the squadron's younger pilots, simply getting the reps is a valuable experience. From joining up with a tanker multiple times, to dynamically managing their fuel for longer sorties, to executing tactics properly in a task saturated environment when they may be exhausted. Even the simple things like using an unfamiliar airfield and talking to unfamiliar controllers.

"As a flight lead or as a wingman, you needed to focus on the details, plan through everything. I want them to see where they were uncomfortable, so that they can focus on those things. If we fail, we want to fail here. That's OK. We'll bring that back home. Focus on those things and get better.

"Red Flag 24-3 provided another chance to pick up and move the squadron and stay proficient at that. The training received at a Red Flag is at a high level, everyone assigned to the squadron got a lot out of the exercise. Squadron pilots lead two missions."

Discussing VMFA-542's mid-term plan, Lt Col Hansell said: "Our first formal seven-month deployment as part of a MEU is scheduled in late 2026. I'm likely to hand over command of VMFA-542 in the summer of 2025, which will give the new commander a year plus to place the squadron on a maritime footing, focused on boat operations."

Left: **An F-35B assigned to VMFA-542 taxies prior to taking off for a mission during Red Flag-Nellis 24-3 at Nellis Air Force Base, Nevada.**
US Air Force/ William Lewis

Left: **US Marines with VMGR-252, refuel an F-35B Lightning II jet assigned to VMFA-542 using aviation-delivered ground refuelling at Kallax Air Base, Sweden during Exercise Nordic Response 24.**
US Marine Corps/ LCpl Orlanys Diaz Figueroa